BELIEVE

BELIEVE

MY FAITH AND THE TACKLE THAT CHANGED MY LIFE

ERIC LeGRAND
with Mike Yorkey

WILLIAM MORROW
An Imprint of HarperCollinsPublishers

Grateful acknowledgment is made to the following for the use of the photographs: insert pages 6 (bottom), 7 (top, bottom left, bottom right), 9 (top, bottom), 16 (bottom) © by Rutgers Athletic Communications; insert page 8 (top) courtesy of the Kessler Institute; insert pages 11 (top left), 12 (top, bottom), 13 (top, middle, bottom), 15 (middle, bottom) © by Sara Partridge; insert page 16 (top) courtesy of Mike Yorkey. All other photographs courtesy of the author.

HarperCollins books may be purchased for educational, business, or sales promotional use. For information please write: Special Markets Department, HarperCollins Publishers, 10 East 53rd Street, New York, NY 10022.

A hardcover edition of this book was published in 2012 by William Morrow, an imprint of HarperCollins Publishers.

FIRST WILLIAM MORROW PAPERBACK EDITION PUBLISHED 2013.

Library of Congress Cataloging-in-Publication Data has been applied for.

ISBN 978-0-06-222631-0

13 14 15 16 17 DIX/RRD 10 9 8 7 6 5 4 3 2 1

To my mother, Karen;
you've been there every step of the way
throughout this incredible journey.
And to the many people who have had my back.

CONTENTS

FOREWORD BY KIRK HERBSTREIT, COLLEGE FOOTBALL AND GAMEDAY ANALYST FOR ABC SPORTS AND ESPN

———

On the morning of Saturday, October 16, 2010, I was in Madison, Wisconsin, making my first visit in six years to the University of Wisconsin campus as part of the ESPN GameDay broadcasting crew. My colleagues Chris Fowler, Lee Corso, Desmond Howard, and I were in Madison for one of those big games between two powerhouse programs: No. 1-ranked Ohio State versus No. 18-ranked Wisconsin.

Inside Camp Randall Stadium, boisterous Badger fans cheered from behind the GameDay set. I knew Wisconsin fans could be rowdy; back in 1992 when I was playing quarterback for Ohio State, a Wisconsin fan nailed me with a flying tomato as I was taking the field.

In between the GameDay broadcast and the start of the night game (which I commented on with play-by-play man Brent Musberger), I watched footage from other college games that played around the country that day. When I viewed a clip of a kickoff play between Rutgers University and Army, I winced. A Rutgers defender had made a big hit and gone down, and the announcer said the injury was serious enough for the player to be carted off the field and taken to a nearby hospital. His name was Eric LeGrand.

Those kind of hits are always hard to watch, and I was hoping that it was one of those stinger injuries that would go away after a day or two. But in the next couple of days, we learned the devastating news that Eric LeGrand was paralyzed from the neck down.

Like millions of college football fans, I have followed Eric's story ever since that afternoon. I have four boys of my own, and I can't begin to imagine what it would be like if one of my sons suffered a similar life-changing injury. My heart went out to Eric and his family.

I've since had the opportunity to visit with Eric over the phone, and everything about him—his upbeat nature, his determined will—was confirmed in our conversation. To talk to a guy who has every reason to be in a bit of a funk, to ask *Why me?*, but who remains so positive left me feeling inspired and greatly impressed. Eric approaches his recovery and his life with profound and magnetic energy. His attitude is contagious; he is one of those guys you want to be around.

I'm just one of many people who have been blown away by how ready Eric is to attack his recovery and how he does not want people to feel sorry for him. His unfaltering faith has a lot to do with that. He sees his life now as a ministry to others.

Having the opportunity to inspire others is what motivates Eric every single day. Just as Eric believes that he will one day leave his wheelchair behind, we have to believe in him, too.

I certainly do. If anyone can beat the odds, it's Eric LeGrand.

BELIEVE

1

THE QUIET BEFORE THE DAWN

I am constantly cold.

My body's been that way ever since my accident.

At one time, my body—when properly clothed—could maintain a constant temperature of approximately 98.6 degrees Fahrenheit, no matter how hot or cold it was outside. My body could adjust to the heat of the sun or the chill in the air.

During the hot summer months, when I was running through a series of football drills at training camp, my body would send a signal to the brain via the spinal cord saying, *Hey, it's getting hot around here! We need to cool things down.* And then I'd start sweating, which was good because perspiration evaporates and cools the skin.

I liked working up a good sweat on the practice field. Dripping perspiration is the body's normal reaction from exposure to hot temperatures and intense physical exercise.

When fall came around, my body reacted to cooler temperatures by prompting my brain to tell me to put on more clothes to keep me warm. Like most kids, I never felt that cold growing up, but my mother made sure I was always wearing a jacket whenever I left the house on chilly days or during a winter cold snap here in New Jersey. Once I got older, all I needed was a couple of layers. I could handle the cold and didn't let it bother me.

But now, with fractured vertebrae in my spinal column, the cold is unbearable. The spinal cord is where a major collection of nerves transmits motor and sensory information to and from the brain to the rest of the body. Any message from the brain must pass through the spinal cord to reach the body's muscles, arms, and legs.

Let's say you have an itch on your nose. A message will journey from your brain, through the nerves in your spinal cord, and reach your right hand in less time than it takes to blink an eye. Once your hand receives that message to scratch your nose, your body takes the correct action to complete the task. No one likes an itchy nose. When the spinal cord is damaged, however, that message from the brain can't get through the tangle of nerves, which means you can't move your hand to satisfy that itch.

Following my accident, the column of nerves that traveled from the brain to the tailbone had gone haywire. My brain was firing messages, but the rest of my body was incapable of receiving them. The result was a sudden and complete loss of movement. I can't walk, I can't move my torso, I can't flex my fingers or toes. And my body can no longer adjust its core temperature. My internal "thermostat" is busted. Because my paralyzed muscles can't move blood around my body like they did when I walked, ran, bent over, or reached up, my blood pools against my skin.

No blood circulation equals no warmth. The result is a perpetual and gnawing sense of cold, kind of like I'm wearing shorts, T-shirt, and flip-flops on a day when the temperatures outside are in the mid to high fifties. I'm not freezing, but it sure feels chilly to me.

Mom keeps the heat inside our apartment at 78 degrees during the day, which is still a few degrees cooler than I'd like, but our home heating bills are high enough as it is. She usually dresses me in training outfits from my old team at Rutgers University and a sweater. If I'm still cold, she turns on a small electric heater in my bedroom. Even with the additional heat, though, I never feel completely warm.

I've told Mom that I wouldn't mind moving to Miami, although I know that's not practical at the moment. But it sure would be nice living where the temperature would be in my sweet spot— somewhere in the mid to high 80s. I currently live in the central area of the Garden State, where the summers are warm but the winters are gray and cold—a damp cold.

In the spring and fall, I rarely go outside in short sleeves and can't be in the shade very long because I need the warmth of the sun. If I go inside a commercial building, though, I don't like the air-conditioning at all, especially if a fan is blowing on me. Restaurants are the worst, especially on hot, sticky days when they crank up the AC to the maximum. During the dog days of August, it feels like I'm eating inside a refrigerator. Sometimes I shiver waiting for my food.

I travel around in a wheelchair-accessible VW Routan van with Mom behind the wheel. As soon as the ramp goes up and the side door closes, I ask Mom to turn up the heat, even on a warm fall day of an Indian summer.

I used to think those clear, sunny afternoons in October made for perfect football weather . . . not too hot, not too cold. I loved the feeling of freedom—free to run with the wind, free to make my own path, and free to knock my opponents to the ground. That's why I loved playing the game of football. My athletic body always felt warm, no matter what the temperature was outside.

Then something happened during a football game that changed my life forever.

Needing a Lift

There are a lot of things I can't do these days, simple things that I took for granted before my accident—like putting myself to bed. Mom, who's my main caregiver, has to perform that chore every night. I weigh 245 pounds—thirty pounds under my playing weight—but I'm still a big load, especially for a mother who's a hundred pounds lighter than me.

In my bedroom we have a hydraulic patient lift—also known as a Hoyer Lift—that uses a sling with straps to move me from my wheelchair to my bed. The toughest part for Mom is lifting up my legs so that she can pull the sling through and position it under me at the same time.

When Mom is satisfied that she has me properly in the sling— and this part usually takes fifteen minutes—she brings over the Hoyer lift, which raises me out of my chair so that she can move me over to my bed. It's kind of like one of those floor cranes you see in car repair shops to lift engines and other heavy parts. After hooking up each strap to the top of the Hoyer Lift, Mom can elevate or lower me as necessary. Mom rolls the lift toward my bed and positions it as close to the bed as she can before lowering me.

Then it's a matter of working me out of the sling, which takes some time since the sling is mostly under my lower back and the top half of my torso. Once she's removed the sling and pushed the Hoyer lift to the side, Mom can help get me ready to go sleep.

She lowers the bed to a lay-flat position and starts by taking off my pants, which must be done one leg at a time. Then she take off my sweater, the top of my training outfit, and whatever shirt I happen to be wearing that day.

I sleep on a microAIR 95 Mattress from Invacare, which automatically turns me every hour so that I won't get bedsores. You don't want to get bedsores because they can kill you. The sore can become infected, and the infection can spread into your bloodstream.

I sleep in my boxers without a shirt on, which you may think is crazy because of how cold I am all the time, but I can't wear an undershirt. I've tried sleeping with a nightshirt, but my shirt would get twisted when the bed turned me to the right or the left. When that happened, I couldn't do anything to fix the predicament I found myself in, which meant I had to call for Mom in the middle of the night. She sleeps in the bedroom next to mine.

When Mom finishes undressing me, she has to change my leg bag. Since I must use a catheter, I wear a collection bag inside my pants. Mom attaches the night bag, which holds more urine, to the side of the bed.

Then she takes off my socks and fluffs up my leg pillow, which keeps my legs elevated and helps keep down the swelling from being in a down position in my wheelchair all day. Every night Mom slides each hand into a leather splint to keep my fingers from curling up while I sleep, another side effect of my spinal cord injury. My hands still lie flat, and I want to keep them that way. That's something I don't want—curled fingers.

Finally Mom secures my trademark long dreadlocks into a ponytail and covers me with a warm blanket, tucking it in behind my shoulders. A lot of times, particularly on cold nights, I'll want my blanket tucked over my head.

Then it's lights out. Mom says that I'm usually snoring within minutes of her turning out the lights and closing my bedroom door.

Every hour, my high-tech mattress moves me into a new position so that I'm not lying on the same pressure points all night long. I usually don't notice that I'm being moved around the first few hours I sleep.

My dreams are strange. In every single one of them, I'm not in my wheelchair. I'm walking around. I haven't forgotten what that feeling is like. Or sometimes I'm running on the beach. I'll be tossing a football with friends, enjoying the salt air and the warm sunshine. It feels so weird because it seems so real. I really think I can catch a football again. *Wow, I can do this.*

Then my bed rotates, and my body moves, which wakes me up a bit. I try to move, and nothing happens. I realize I was just dreaming. But I don't let myself get down. I tell myself, *Maybe it's not today. Maybe it's another day.* I know one day it will shockingly happen. Maybe I'll be able to lift a finger, or maybe I'll be able to lift one of my arms. When that happens, everyone will be surprised. I'm waiting for that day to come. I know God has a plan for something like that.

I fall back asleep, and the dreams start all over again. I'll be walking again, or lifting up a spoonful of ice cream to eat, but around four or five o'clock in the morning, I stir from being automatically turned around again. There's not much else I can do except to lay half awake in the darkness, surrounded by my thoughts. It's at those times when my mind takes me to places that I don't want to revisit—like that horrible afternoon at Giants Stadium.

The date is etched in my memory: October 16, 2010.

———

We were playing Army at the Meadowlands, and we were down a touchdown, 17–10, with ten minutes to go in the fourth quarter. The Black Knights were on our 46-yard line, but they faced a third-and-eight to keep their drive going.

"Time for a stop!" yelled my buddy, linebacker Antonio Lowery, as we broke from our huddle. Army had three first downs on this drive, and they were marching down the field. We had to hold them to keep it a one-score game.

I was a nose guard, the player who lined up off the center. At

275 pounds, I usually gave up a good twenty-five to thirty pounds to the beefy dudes on the front line. But our head coach, Greg Schiano, liked his defensive lineman to be a tad smaller and a lot quicker, and that's where I fit in.

I took my three-point stance and remembered from our film sessions one of Army's plays. They would pull their guard and the fullback would try to take our defensive linemen out, opening a big hole for their running back, Jared Hassin, who, at six feet, three inches and 235 pounds, liked to square up his shoulders and run north-south. Hassin was tough to bring down when he had a head of steam behind him; he had already run on us for 100 yards.

Both teams lined up for this big third-down play, and I awaited the snap of the ball. Their quarterback, Trent Steelman, was going through his cadence as players moved in motion before the hike of the ball. I sensed something, so I shifted over a yard or two to place myself into the gap between the guard and the center hiking the ball. Sure enough, on the hike of the ball, the guard went out, but instead of following him, I maintained my ground for a split second and then shot through the gap, slipping past the other guard who was assigned to block me.

Suddenly, I was in the Army backfield, and their quarterback handed the ball off to Hassin. I popped him pretty good in the chest and nailed him to the ground for a one-yard loss. It was a good hit.

I pulled myself up to celebrate, but my head was buzzing. I saw some stars. My teammate Scott Vallone, a six-foot, three-inch defensive tackle, was going crazy with joy, giving me a chest bump as my other teammates came over to congratulate me. But I had been dinged. I guess I hit Hassin with my head because my bell had been rung.

Feeling woozier by the second, I went on autopilot. It was fourth down. I knew I had to get off the field. I started trudging toward the sideline—and looked up to see nothing but white uniforms and gold helmets.

What's going on? Then it hit me. I was going the wrong way. I was making my way toward the Army sideline!

"Hey, Eric!" Scott yelled amid the confusion.

This wasn't my sideline. I had to go the other way. Knowing that I was running out of time, I began sprinting back to our bench before Army snapped the ball.

No one on our sideline noticed that I had been going the wrong way on an exit ramp. Several happy coaches came over and tapped me on the helmet. "Good job!" each of them yelled, fired up because we had made a crucial fourth-quarter stop in a close game.

I found a place on the bench and took off my helmet. Maybe I had a slight concussion out there on the field. No, that wasn't it. I had had a concussion playing football one time—back in Junior Pee Wees during my Pop Warner days—and this wasn't a concussion.

I drank some water and took a few minutes to catch my breath. Then our fans started cheering like crazy. An Army punt had us pinned back at the 7-yard line, but D. C. Jefferson caught a long ball for a 53-yard gain to the Army 43-yard line. Eight plays later, QB Chas Dodd hit Mark Harrison with a 16-yard touchdown pass, and we were back in it: 17–17.

"Kickoff team!" yelled our special teams coach, Robb Smith.

That was my cue. In addition to playing defense for half the snaps, I was a special-teamer, a member of the "bomb squad" on kickoff coverage. My job was to sprint down the field while the ball was in the air and annihilate any blockers, fill any running lanes, and knock the kick returner to the ground. Those who were part of the kickoff coverage team played with a lot of spirit and reckless abandon. You had to play that way because a tackle deep in your opponent's territory—like inside the 20-yard line—often set the tone for the next series of plays.

I took my position next to our kicker, San San Te, who had a good leg. I was to his immediate left.

We were set. The head referee in a black-and-white vertically striped shirt and white knickers blew his whistle and circled his right arm, and our fans rose to their feet. My heart rate always notched up several levels for kickoff.

San San took several mincing steps, and I let him pass. He was about to plant his left foot when a gust of wind blew the ball off the tee.

Time to reload.

San San reset the ball on the tee, and on the next whistle by the referee, his kick lofted into the autumn air.

Little did I know that everything about my life was about to change.

2

WHERE MY STORY STARTS

Life can change in the flash of an eye.

I didn't know that concept very well growing up, but Mom sure did.

I was a three-year-old preschooler when my uncle, James Edward LeGrand Jr., and his girlfriend had gone into Manhattan for a jazz concert on a Saturday night. They were driving home at 2 A.M. on the New Jersey Turnpike when they came up on Exit 12—their exit.

Uncle Jimmy was at the wheel of his Isuzu Trooper when a drunk driver plowed into the back of his car. Unfortunately, my uncle wasn't wearing his seat belt, and the collision threw him out of the SUV, which rolled over and landed on top of him, killing him. His girlfriend survived, but it took her nearly a year of physical therapy before she healed. She wasn't wearing her seat belt, either.

Mom said her brother's tragic death hit the family hard. He was only thirty-two years old, with a lot of life to live. My grandmother, Betty Jean, continually asked herself, *Why him?* His death was quite a shock to my family, who had lost my grandfather, James

Edward LeGrand Sr., only three and a half years earlier. He died of lung cancer at the age of fifty, just four months before I was born.

After the accident, there was always a sense of something missing during the holidays. I was quite young at the time, so I didn't understand the significance of Uncle Jimmy's loss, but Mom would tell me about my uncle as well as my grandfather and how they were wonderful men. The death of her father and the sudden loss of her brother was a vivid reminder to Mom that life can change just like that—in the blink of an eye. I also learned that in a moment everything could be taken away from you, but what I didn't understand at the time—and *couldn't* understand—was how an event later in my life would prove just that.

It was through these tragedies that Mom persevered. She taught me that life goes on and the importance of a positive outlook. Mom and I are very close. She has always been my number-one fan on the sidelines and away from the playing field. She has worked to give me a good life even though it hasn't always been easy.

No One Could Catch Her

My mom, Karen, comes from Colonia, New Jersey, which is the next town over from Avenel, where we've lived since I was four years old. Mom's family moved to Colonia from nearby Elizabeth in the mid-1960s, when Colonia was a quiet small town with dirt roads. Education was a top priority for her parents, and Colonia's schools had a good reputation.

Mom was the oldest of three children. Uncle Jimmy came next, followed by my aunt Cheryl, who's eight years younger than my mother. Mom went to elementary school, junior high, and high school in Colonia and was quite athletic, excelling at track, basketball, and softball. Recently an old classmate found Mom on

Facebook and messaged her: "Karen, do you remember when we were in sixth grade and you were the fastest girl in school, I was the fastest boy, and we raced each other? I barely beat you that day."

None of the girls could catch Mom, and only a few boys were brave enough to take her on in a fifty-yard sprint back in sixth grade. But when she started Colonia High, she gave up track to play basketball and softball. She wasn't a girly girl, but she wasn't a tomboy, either. She was a girl athlete at a time when there weren't many.

She told me that her father, James Sr., was a no-nonsense type of dad. All it took was one look from him and you shaped up. Mom and her siblings used to call his serious face "the stare." They knew that when he gave them the stare, it was time to stop messing around. But most of the time, my grandfather had a smile on his face and was fun to be with.

My grandmother, Betty, whom I call Nana and is still with us today, wasn't as strict as my grandfather. If my mother did something wrong and her father punished or grounded her, she would go to Nana and plead her case. My grandmother would usually give in if her daughter begged long enough.

Maybe that's because Mom was consistently an obedient child who took care of her younger sister, Cheryl, every day after school. Nana worked eight-to-five on the assembly line at Revlon, the cosmetics company, and my grandfather covered the late shift as an operations manager at Wakefern Food Corporation, where he worked graveyard from 11 P.M. to 7 A.M. During her high school years, Mom would do Cheryl's hair in the morning, fix her lunch, and look after her when she came home from school since her father was often asleep until late in the afternoon. Even when Mom wanted to see friends, she would have to take her little sister along. She also had to keep an eye on Jimmy.

Mom always tells me how tough she had it growing up, from taking care of her siblings to having to walk to class every morning.

There was no such thing as a warm car ride to school on a cold morning, not in the LeGrand household. Her parents felt the discipline of walking to school every day would teach her and her brother and sister responsibility. Mom learned to do things without complaining. You get on with life, and that's sometimes the way things are.

Mom was a straight-A student in high school but not the studious type. Her best sport was basketball, which she had played competitively since seventh grade. But on a snowy January day during her senior year, in the middle of basketball season, she was stepping out of the car when she slipped on a patch of black ice. She fell hard and broke her ankle. She was devastated. Her days of playing basketball were over.

Mom says she wasn't good enough to play hoops in college anyway, but we'll never know. Not sure what she wanted to do with her life, she enrolled at nearby Rutgers University, just twenty minutes away in New Brunswick. She was put on a waiting list for housing, but students who lived farther away were given priority, so Mom had to live at home and rely on public transportation to get to Rutgers. One time she fell asleep, missed her stop, and had to call my great-grandmother to come get her.

It turned out that attending college just wasn't Mom's thing, so she dropped out of Rutgers after one semester. She wanted to work. She wanted to make money. She wanted to be independent and get a place of her own.

Her parents weren't happy to hear her change of heart, and I'm sure her father gave her "the stare." Mom got the message and quickly found a job as a receptionist at Gordon's Gin and Vodka in Linden, New Jersey. She was nineteen years old, and this was her very first paycheck. At the time, she was seeing a guy she knew from high school. They had been dating for several years when she became pregnant. It wasn't planned, and she was nervous about telling my grandparents the news.

When she finally revealed to them that she was expecting, her parents told her, *We're behind you*, but in the same breath they reminded my mom that the life inside her was her responsibility. "I'm not going to raise your child. You're going to raise your child," Nana told her.

So that's what she did after my older sister, Nicole, was born. Mom said she had always thought she was mature, but having a child was a reality check. Unfortunately, things did not work out with the father, and raising Nicole as a single parent made my mother grow up in a hurry. She became both a mom and a dad to Nicole. Since she needed to provide for her daughter's needs, Mom had to go back to work at Gordon's two months after she gave birth. A friend of my grandmother's who babysat children took care of Nicole in her home.

A few years later, Mom and Nicole moved to Elizabeth, New Jersey, which was more urban. Mom felt there would be more opportunities there for her, and she landed a new job in Jersey City. But she kept Nicole with a babysitter back in Colonia, in the suburbs. Mom didn't want her daughter to be a city kid, which is why she eventually moved back to the Colonia area.

My Introduction

Nicole was around five years old when Mom started dating my father, Donald McCloud. Six years later at the age of thirty-one, Mom became pregnant with me. I was born on September 4, 1990, at Elizabeth General Hospital.

My parents didn't get married, but they lived together for the first five years of my life. Mom, however felt she was cast again in the role as the mother and the father in the relationship, and she wanted Nicole and me to grow up with her values and her morals. She wanted us to believe in God and learn the Golden Rule—treating others as we would want to be treated.

I remember one time when I was in first or second grade, and I came home with a clenched fist. "What's in your hand?" Mom asked.

I opened my hand and showed her a half-dozen plastic tire valve caps.

"Where did you get those?"

"Ah, I took them off cars."

"What's wrong with you, boy?" She turned me right around and opened the front door. "Eric, you go back and you put those caps back on every single car that you took them off of."

That wasn't going to fly in Mom's house. She wanted me to learn the same strong work ethic that she had been taught by her father and mother. My grandparents—and subsequently my mother—believed that nothing was given to you, not in this life.

Mom was also determined that her children would not make some of the same mistakes she had made. She told me in no uncertain terms: "You go to high school, you go to college, you finish college, and then you get a good job. You live the right way."

I was heading into first grade when my father moved out, the same year Mom purchased—with my grandmother's help—our first home in Avenel, a multiracial community of seventeen thousand within Woodbridge Township in Middlesex County.

Avenel is a real melting pot with a strong sense of community—about half the population is white, 20 percent is African-American, 20 percent is Asian, and 10 percent is Hispanic. Mom felt Avenel would be a great place to raise an energetic young boy.

I was certainly energetic in those early years. You might say I was as spirited as a young colt and just as strong willed. I wanted what I wanted from early on and was determined to get it. I usually gave Mom a hard time because I was so stubborn. There were occasions when I'd exasperate Mom so much she'd pick the phone to call her sister. "Cheryl, come get him," she'd say. "If you don't come get him, I'm gonna kill him. I don't want to do that, so just come get him and take him away for a little bit so I can calm myself down."

I was frequently raising Mom's blood pressure as a kid, but she likes to tell one story in particular. When we were living in an apartment in nearby Woodbridge, the top floor had a finished attic, where I slept in a crib next to Mom's bed. Nicole slept downstairs in the other bedroom.

I was a toddler, two or three years old, when one day I decided I was going to ride my toy horse down the steep wooden stairs. Mom tried to stop me, but in a flash I pointed my toy pony down the stairs and pushed off. I'm told that I lasted for about three steps before tumbling down the stairs and landing in a heap.

Mom chased after me, scared to death about what shape I'd be in on the landing, but I was fine. I didn't cry. I just wanted to find out what my limits were.

It seems that I tested my limits pretty regularly when I was young, like the time I collected fireflies in a glass jar back in elementary school. Mom put holes in the top of the aluminum lid so the fireflies could breathe and gave me explicit instructions not to bring the fireflies into the house. "Leave them outside in the backyard," Mom sternly warned.

Well, I decided that my menagerie of fireflies wasn't getting enough air on a particularly warm summer evening, so I brought them inside and made the air holes bigger. I was in my bedroom, laying on my bed, and the next thing I knew, I heard Mom screaming from her bedroom, where she was watching TV. I ran in to see what the commotion was about, and she said, "Look at all the fireflies!"

Sure enough, those creatures were flying around Mom's semi-dark bedroom, emitting their light and circling her bed. Mom got after me pretty good that night.

Mom wasn't the only person whose patience I tried. I didn't like to listen to my older sister, even though she was a *lot* older than me. When I was four and Nicole was fifteen and in high school, she babysat me and had the unenviable task of putting me to bed. I gave her my typical hard time—I didn't want to go to bed and was in no mood to obey my older sister.

"You will do what I say!" Nicole retorted.

"No, I won't!" I fired back.

We got into a tussle when she tried to pick me up and physically enforce her order. I fought back even though there was a wide age gap and physical difference. I was such a strong little kid that Nicole couldn't take me. The only way she established order that night was by sitting on me. That's where she put her weight advantage to good use.

Nicole will tell you that I was a brat. If she told me that I had to eat dinner before Mom came home to take me to Pop Warner football practice, I told her I didn't want to eat dinner. Then she'd repeat her order, and I'd cross my arms and shake my head. I used to think I was the "man of the house" when Mom left, and that meant I had to be a little tough guy.

Testing Mom

We had moved to Avenel a few months before I started kindergarten. I can still remember standing on a jungle gym in our backyard—the gym was about six feet high—and looking over the fence and seeing the other boys in the neighborhood play. Every weekend, I used to stand there for hours watching them go up and down the street, riding their bikes or throwing a ball around.

"Why don't you go out there and ask them to play with you?" Mom asked a few weeks after we moved in.

I was all embarrassed, but Mom finally convinced me to knock on one of their doors.

I knew where this one kid lived, so I gathered my courage and walked to the house down the street. A mother answered my knock. "Do you have any kids I can play with?" I asked.

"Sure, young man," and that's how I came to know Joey Brannigan, Doug Tobias, and Charlie Schwartz, and we became thick as thieves all through elementary school. Joey and Dougie were my age, but Charlie was five years older than us, so he was our leader. They were all white, but you know, back then colors didn't mean anything. We just got together and had fun playing in my sandbox, riding our bikes, and building ramps for jumps. My daredevil days had not ended with riding a trike down a wooden stairwell.

If it was Dougie, Joey, and me, then we would play with our Matchbox cars or play tag or Manhunt. But when Charlie came around, we usually played a game called "Kill the man with the ball." You can figure out the object of that game.

Whatever we were doing, Charlie showed no mercy on us. When we were older and started played basketball in one of the driveways and someone went in for a layup, Charlie would send him flying into the basketball pole or garage door. That hurt!

Charlie told us to be tough. "Don't cry," he'd say. "Get back up."

Since Charlie was the oldest, we always tried to impress him, so we dusted ourselves off and got back into the game. You couldn't complain. That was an unwritten rule in my neighborhood.

During the first few years of elementary school, I went to the

Little Fiddler day-care center after school because Mom had to work, and I knew I had no choice. Little Fiddler was next door to my elementary school, so one of the teachers would pick me up when class was over.

In fourth grade, though, I decided I was too big for Little Fiddler.

"Ma, I don't want to go to day care any longer," I announced one day as we ate dinner. "I'm bigger than everyone else at Little Fiddler. I want to just come home after school."

Mom thought for a minute. Even though I was the youngest in my fourth-grade class, I was still the biggest kid. "All right. We'll try this," she said, and Mom gave me a plan. Each morning, she gave me a key to the house with instructions that I was to take the school bus home and then call her at work as soon as I stepped inside the front door. And then I would have to stay inside until she got home.

By this time, Nicole had gone to North Carolina A&T State University, a historically black college in Greensboro, North Carolina, where she had chosen biology as her major. Nicole was a smart student who wanted to become a scientist, but she wasn't around to look after me while Mom was still at work.

I was good about following Mom's directions to stay in the house after school, but I still tested my limits, frequently calling Mom at work:

"Can Dougie come over? We're just going to watch some TV."

"No, Eric. I don't want anyone coming into the house."

Then I would make five more phone calls to her, each a variation of the previous one. I wouldn't give up until she said, "Okay, Eric, fine. Dougie can come over, but no one else."

Sometimes Mom didn't give in, and I could hear it in her voice that enough was enough. Then I would leave her alone. But when she did give in, she would say, "I'm giving you all the freedom in the world, but if you do something wrong, I will pull in the rope. If you hang yourself, that's it. It's over."

I understood, and behaved, waiting patiently until she returned from work. But when she did get home, especially during the daylight savings months, I was all over the neighborhood. I usually played basketball in someone's driveway or joined in pick-up football games in the park.

"I understand you're playing, but I need to know where you are," Mom said one day.

"Yes, Mom."

I tried to be better, but then I would get so caught up playing basketball with my friends that I wouldn't even come home for dinner.

Finally, Mom got me one of those prepaid phones. "This phone is for me," she said. "When I call you, you come home."

The problem was that Mom was always breaking up a good basketball or football game. I was a social kid and wanted to be with my friends and play outside from sunup to sundown, so if Mom didn't let me go out and play, I'd moan and complain to get my way. Mom had a spirited child on her hands, but fortunately she found an outlet for my energy by getting me involved in sports at an early age. From the time I started kindergarten, I was able to learn lessons about life on and off the field.

The Youngest and the Biggest

Birthdays were always a big deal for me. Maybe it was because September 4 always fell around Labor Day and was the last big summer holiday before school started.

Because of my September birthday, I was four years old when

I entered kindergarten, which made me the youngest in my class. I suppose Mom could have held me back, but I was already bigger than all the other kids, even though many of them were six, nine, or even ten months older than me. This set a pattern that would follow me right into college.

Just before I started kindergarten, Mr. Tobias told Mom that he was going to sign up Doug for Pop Warner football and thought I should play too because of my size. Mom thought putting me into Pop Warner football was a great idea. Since I had tons of energy, why not burn a few calories running up and down a football field?

I started playing in the Pop Warner flag division just before I turned five in September. Once again I was one of the youngest players in a division for five-, six-, and seven-year-olds, which had a weight limit of seventy-five pounds.

In Pop Warner flag football, no tackling was allowed. You ran until another player grabbed one of the flags on a belt around your waist. The coaches were going to put me on the line because of my size, but when they saw me run, they had second thoughts. They moved me to running back because I was so fast.

Football was pretty simple when all us kids were little shrimps. The head coach usually told me to take the handoff from the quarterback and run around the corner. That's what I always did, and most kids weren't fast enough to catch me.

Mom liked me playing Pop Warner and never missed a play. She also put me into Little League baseball, and when I got a little older, I started playing youth basketball, too. I liked all three sports, and at a young age, I didn't have a favorite.

After two seasons of flag football when I was just about to turn seven, I finally got to play *real* football in the Mitey-Mites division of Pop Warner. Helmets and pads. Tackling to the ground. Football became a lot more serious, even if we were only seven or eight years old. At least, that's how the coaches made us feel. They had us practice a lot . . . several times a week. And then we had our games every Saturday.

I didn't understand why I had to practice so much. I'd rather just play in the games than practice. But Mom told me that once you commit to something, you commit to it 100 percent. You can't just show up on game days and expect to play.

Get your uniform on, she'd say. When I would still give her a hard time, she would remind me about the commitment I made to the team. "You do not miss practices. You will not do that."

I got the message, and it contributed to the development of a strong work ethic, which has helped tremendously with my rehabilitation efforts. I grew up knowing that you practice every single day. You give it your all in training, and then you play the game. That's the reward, stepping onto the field.

In the Mitey-Mites, the coaches placed me at running back and safety. Mom didn't understand why I was playing safety because when she looked at the safety position in the colleges and pros, he was the guy covering the receivers when they go long. I told her that the safety in Pop Warner was more like playing linebacker. I did make a lot of tackles in Pop Warner, so what I said made sense.

When I played on the offensive side of the ball, I was a tough runner to bring down. I'd usually drag three kids down the field, even though they grabbed my legs and ankles and hung on for dear life. I would just keep my legs moving, I was too big for them to take down. I'm sure it was an amusing sight to watch.

My mom truly was my number-one fan. Every time I took off on a long running play toward the end zone, my mother would run down the sideline alongside me, yelling, *Go! Go!* She was crazy out there, running down the field and cheering me on while I was sprinting for the end zone. The other parents got a laugh out of it and would tease her every time she chased after me, but Mom says she let the adrenaline get the best of her. Besides, she was too antsy to sit still.

A lot of parents came to the game to talk and socialize, but they knew Mom wasn't into chitchatting with those who joined her on the sidelines. Her body language said, *Don't talk to me. I'm watching the game.* She understood what was going on. She was very much into football. When our offense moved down the field, she moved with us and kept her eyes on the ball. And when I took the football and turned the corner, she was running right behind me, cheering as I took the ball to the house.

I never witnessed Mom running behind me while I was making a long run to the end zone because I was too busy looking to see if any defenders were going to catch me. It's a good thing, too, because I probably would have stopped in the middle of my run, put my hands on my hips, and said to her, "Are you kidding me?"

Always in My Corner

What Mom saw in me early on was a passion for football. I loved the rough-and-tumble play, and as I got older, I identified with the warrior mind-set even though off the field, I was easygoing and friendly. They used to call me the "gentle giant" back in elementary school. I didn't get into fights, and I didn't bully people even though I was one of the biggest kids in my class.

Throughout my Pop Warner days, there was nothing that would keep me off the field, not even an injury. At the end of one game, I came over to the sideline and showed Mom my right elbow, which was ten times the normal size.

"That looks horrible," Mom said. "How did that happen?"

"I don't know how I hurt my elbow. But it doesn't bother me."

"Did you show your coaches?"

"No. I didn't want them to take me out."

You see, I had a very high pain tolerance, which I displayed early on during a visit to the doctor's office. When my pediatrician announced that it was time to get a booster shot, I didn't flinch when she took a syringe out of the drawer and showed me the needle.

In fact, I was curious how a syringe worked, so I watched the doctor jab my left bicep with the hypodermic needle and push on the plunger to deliver the medicine. I didn't make a sound or a cry.

Nor did I cry when I busted my big toe playing kickball in sixth grade. What bothered me more was knowing that I had a big track meet the following day. All the area schools in Woodbridge Township were competing in a variety of running and jumping events.

I limped home, and when Mom looked at the big toe on my right foot, she was shocked at how black and blue the swollen joint was. She immediately iced it, telling me that there was no way I was running in that track meet. We continued icing, and then in the morning, Mom wrapped up the toe.

"Do you think I'll be able to run today?" I asked Mom.

"You can barely walk as it is," she replied. "I don't see how you're going to be much better by this afternoon."

When it came time to run the fifty-yard dash, I was at the starting line. The starter's gun went off, and I finished second against the fastest kids. All with a broken toe.

I loved competition, so when it came to injury or adversity, I was going to overcome pain or bad breaks. I felt like nothing could stop me.

3

A WEIGHTY PROBLEM AND

A HEFTY ATTITUDE

Even though I was a handful growing up, Mom learned how to use that to her advantage at times.

It was in fifth grade that I began my obsession with sneakers. I was flipping through the pages of an Eastbay sports catalog, and my eyes landed on the most beautiful pair in the world: the Nike Air Hyperflights.

I'm talking about jaw-dropping, flashy kicks that looked like they just landed here from Mars. NBA stars Jason Williams, Damon Stoudamire, and Derek Fisher were wearing them, and they were so cool. They came in assorted colors, including a shiny, eye-popping cherry-red upper shell and black trim. These sneakers practically screamed, *Hey, look at me!*

I wanted to be the coolest kid in the neighborhood, the envy of Joey, Dougie, and Charlie. And those shoes would make me just that. But when I looked at the price in the catalog, my heart sank. Eastbay wanted $130 for a pair.

I showed Mom the catalog and pointed to the red sneakers. "Mom, can you get me a pair? I'll take care of them. I promise."

Mom rolled her eyes and gave me one of those *Are you kidding me?* looks. "I'm not buying a hundred-and-thirty-dollar pair of shoes just so you can go and dog them up in a week or two," she said.

"No, Mom, I won't mess them up. I'll be real careful when I go outside. I promise."

Mom hesitated, which I knew was a good sign. She was thinking about it.

"Please, Mom. They're great shoes."

"Well, if you want a pair that badly, you're going to have to earn them."

"What do you mean I have to earn them?"

"Tell you what. If you bring home good grades on your next two tests, then we'll see."

I took that as a yes. I didn't usually get the best grades, but from then on, I made sure I paid attention in class and studied extra hard. When I brought home an A and a B on my next two tests, I figured I was in the clear.

Mom studied my test results, then met my eyes. "Let me think about it," she said.

That wasn't good enough. "What do you mean, you'll think about it? You told me if I bring home good grades for a week, I could get the shoes, and I did just that."

It wasn't easy earning those grades either. I had attention problems and was used to socializing in class rather than paying attention. Once the sneakers were on the line, though, I shaped up. Mom hesitated again. "I need two more weeks of good grades," she said.

Well, those two weeks turned into a whole semester. When my report card arrived in the mail, I had one B and the rest were A's. Mom saw that her little "reward" system worked, so true to her word, she got me my pair of Nike Air Hyperflights. The red beauties could be spotted a block away.

I wore my Hyperflights to class every day. Some of the kids teased me because they were so bright, but I didn't care what anyone said. I knew I had worked hard to get those shoes. It was good for me to set a goal, exert myself to attain it, and see the reward. I loved the feeling of accomplishment after putting so much effort into something and seeing it happen.

I didn't wear my red sneakers on the football field, of course, where Mom made sure I wore good cleats. After playing two years of Mitey-Mites, the next division up was called Junior Pee Wee, which was for eight-, nine-, and ten-year-olds who didn't weigh more than 105 pounds. At the age of eight, I was *barely* under the weight limit for Junior Pee Wees, but by the time I was about to turn nine, I had blown past 105 pounds and had to move up to the Pee Wee division, where players weighed between 75 and 120 pounds. In Pee Wees, players could be a year older—eleven years of age.

This would set a pattern throughout Pop Warner football where I would always be playing against kids who were one or two years older than me, because I was too big for my peers. I didn't mind being one of the youngest players on the field, however. I figured that playing against older, heavier opponents improved my game and raised my level of performance.

Touchdown Treats

Even while playing against older, bigger kids, I still gave Mom plenty of reasons to chase me down the sideline. Mom rewarded me for scoring touchdowns by baking me my favorite chocolate chip cookies. I'd set a paper napkin on the kitchen counter next to a glass of milk, and I'd place one warm cookie on each corner and a fifth cookie in the center. Eating them in this manner was one of my great childhood pleasures.

Hitting home runs got the homemade chocolate chip dessert treatment as well. I played a lot of baseball games in elementary and middle school and loved the sport as much as football. Sometimes we had either practice or a game every day from March to June.

I had a good birthday for Little League baseball, where the cut-off date was August 1. (That was changed to May 1 in 2006.) This meant I was one of the *oldest* ten-year-olds or twelve-year-olds on the team. The other good news about Little League baseball was that there was no weight limit, so I was also one of the biggest kids out there.

Even though I also played center fielder, pitching the ball is what really excited me about the grand old game. Standing on the mound and going one-on-one with the batter fired up my competitive juices. I wanted to strike everyone and took it as an insult if someone got a hit off me.

During one game, I was brought in at the bottom of the sixth and last inning with the bases loaded and no outs. I had to protect a one-run lead.

Give me the ball. That was my attitude.

I straddled the rubber and got into the zone by humming a 50 Cent song I heard on the radio that morning. Even though the pressure was on, I went about my business. I didn't want to let my team down.

I may have looked cool on the outside, but pitching consumed me. When baseball season started in the spring, that's all I thought about. I can remember sitting in class on the days I was going to pitch, and my mind was a zillion miles away from my school work. I couldn't pay attention to anything the teacher was saying. I'd spend half my time daydreaming about the game and the other half looking outside to see if the weather would hold. I hated rainouts.

Batters were scared to get into the box against me because I threw the ball fast and was big for my age, standing five feet, eight inches, at twelve years old. From my perch on the mound, I reamed the ball in there, over 70 miles per hour according to the radar gun—a pretty impressive speed considering the pitcher's rubber was only forty-six feet from the plate. My catcher would wear a dirt-bike glove inside his mitt because my fastball stung his hand so bad.

My dream, like every other kid who played baseball, was to make it to Williamsport, Pennsylvania, site of the Little League World Series. Our Woodbridge Township all-star team made a good run at getting there. We won the district and section levels, and then in the state championship, we needed to beat Toms River—a New Jersey team that had won the Little League World Series in Williamsport five years earlier when they beat Kashima, Japan, in the ESPN-televised final. If we defeated Toms River for the 2003 state championship, then we'd go on to the Mid-Atlantic Regional tournament and be just one step from Williamsport.

I pitched the game to get us into the final round with Toms River during pool play. But after that I was out of innings—Little League pitchers are allowed to pitch only six innings a week, to save their arms. I couldn't pitch in the next game against Toms River, and we needed to win to keep our hopes for Williamsport alive.

The game was tied in the bottom of the sixth inning with Toms River at bat. They had a runner on third with two outs when their batter hit a lazy fly ball to our right fielder. If he caught the ball, we would go into extra innings.

I watched in horror as the pop fly bounced off our right fielder's glove, and the winning run scored easily. Our Williamsport dreams were over.

I ran off the field from my center field position and threw my glove against the back of the dugout wall. Then I sat down and bawled my eyes out. I thought the world had come to an end. Mom couldn't console me.

This was the first and only time I ever cried after a game. I was beyond devastated, but there was still a consolation game to play. I was eligible to pitch in that game, which we won with me firing away. But the disappointment from losing the day before took a while to get over. We were a bunch of twelve-year-olds who really thought we were on our way to Williamsport, where we'd play for the ESPN cameras and become famous.

But that's not the lasting legacy of that team. The parents and the players really got to know each other well during that great run for Williamsport, and today many of those parents are the folks who formed the Eric LeGrand Foundation after I went down. Their help has made a tremendous difference in our lives. They were the ones who have stood by us from the very beginning.

Growth Spurt

Throughout the middle school years, I played in youth basketball leagues in winter, Little League baseball in the spring and summer, and Pop Warner in the fall, but I ran into a problem as I was entering eighth grade, which was my last year of eligibility for Pop Warner football.

I weighed too much. That summer before the season started, I tipped the scales at 165 pounds. I had also gone through a growth spurt and stood five feet, eleven inches with the squeakiest voice ever. I had grown so fast that my shoe size went from an 8 to a 12 in a year, and I leapfrogged past several shoe sizes. Those red Nike Hyperflights in my closet looked like little kid shoes. It did get wearisome hearing people say, "My, you're really growing, Eric!" But I loved being taller than my peers.

My weight presented a problem for Pop Warner football since the weight limit for the Midget division was 145 pounds. That limit was raised to 170 pounds in 2012, but back in 2003, I'd have to lose twenty pounds if I wanted to play another season.

My Pop Warner coach, Jack Nevins, was like a father figure to me. When I told him about my weight problem, he was very understanding. "You know, you don't have to do this," he said. "You can start lifting and get ready for high school football next year."

But I couldn't imagine going a whole season without playing football. "No, Coach, this is something I really wanna do. I want to play. This is what I love to do."

"All right," he said. "But it's not going to be easy losing that much weight, especially for a growing boy like you."

I was super motivated, though. I talked to Mom about going on some type of diet and ramping up my exercise program. We decided that I'd go on a Slim-Fast diet where I'd have a Slim-Fast shake for breakfast and lunch, and then I'd eat a healthy dinner without snacking during the day or having dessert after dinner. For exercise, I decided to run four miles a day on a treadmill that we had in the basement. Two miles in the morning, two at night.

You should have seen me working over that poor treadmill. I nearly wore off the moving belt. It was so hot in August, the basement turned into a sauna. Then I really ramped things up by putting on a T-shirt, two sweatshirts, two pairs of sweatpants, two pairs of socks, *and* a black plastic garbage bag underneath my sweatpants. With a garbage bag and so many layers of clothes on my body, I heated up on the treadmill like a Thanksgiving turkey being cooked in a plastic bag. The sweat poured off in buckets.

Sometimes I'd run outside after dinner—still wearing a garbage bag under two pairs of sweatpants—with my friends Doug Tobias, Jerry Venterelli, and Ralph Eastman. They joined me because they also had to lose a few pounds to make weight, so we tried to have some fun with it.

Ralph was a tall, skinny kid from Africa who moved here when he was in the fourth grade. He weighed right around 150 pounds and had to lose five pounds, but I seriously think he had things tougher than I did because he was already skin and bones.

Jerry Venterelli was a different story. He was a chubby Italian kid who could make anyone laugh. He ate too much pizza and cannelloni, so he had a good fifteen pounds to lose. Dougie had a bit of a tire around his waist, too.

Losing twenty pounds in eighth grade just so I could play football wasn't easy, but I did drop all that weight and became eligible to play Midgets. Losing that weight gave me great deal of confidence and determination. I proved to myself that I could make sacrifices (even giving up Mom's homemade chocolate cookies and brownies) to keep my weight under 145 pounds during the season.

To maintain my weight—we had weekly weigh-ins—I became obsessed with the scale in our bathroom. I must have stepped on it two or three times a day, and each time Mom would say, "Eric, don't weigh yourself so much," but I couldn't help it. I had to know where I stood.

Sometimes the pressure to keep my weight under the limit showed up in my attitude on the football field. One time at practice, I got into a pushing match with Nate Brown. Coach Jack had to separate us, but Nate and I had a history that dated back to fifth grade recess. We were playing kickball in the schoolyard and our team was down two runs with the recess bell about to ring. The bases were loaded, and I was up. If I gave the ball a good kick, we'd tie the game and maybe even win it.

But Nate wouldn't roll the ball up the plate. In fact, he held on to the ball and refused to pitch to me.

"Pitch the ball!" I screamed.

"No!" he yelled back, cradling the reddish rubber ball in his arm.

"You punk! Let me kick it!"

Nate held the ball for nearly five minutes as players from both sides screamed at him. Then the recess bell went off, and we ended up losing the game.

Nate and I were both super competitive. During this one particular fight at practice, we gave each other some good shoves. I was ready to throw a punch, but something inside told me to drop my arms and let it go. When Nate saw me back off, he relaxed as well. I flashed a smile, and he returned a smile. Believe it or not, that was the start of a beautiful friendship.

Today, Nate is one of those people who has stood by me during some of my most difficult moments. I'm glad our friendship hasn't changed one little bit over the years.

A Valuable Lesson

While I saw Coach Jack as a father figure, the other coaches—Coach Cheesy and Coach Seaford (I have no idea what their real names or last names were)—were high school students, so I figured they wanted to make the lives of little eighth graders miserable.

They would make us run laps for what seemed like no reason or do bear crawls for what seemed like the slightest mess-up or tiny infraction. If they didn't like our attitude, they'd stop practice and order us to do wind sprints.

One time, Coach Jack wasn't at practice, so Coach Cheesy and Coach Seaford were in charge. We were winning nearly all our games and having a great season, so I thought we could afford to slack off a bit. In fact, that was the general attitude among my teammates.

Not Coach Cheesy and Coach Seaford. They sensed the lack of effort, so they made everyone on the team—including Nate, Ralph,

Doug, and me—run extra laps at the end of practice. I whispered to my teammates, *I'm gonna come in last.* A lot of guys followed my slow pace.

After we had taken our sweet time around the football field, Coach Cheesy and Coach Seaford announced that practice wasn't over.

"Line up on the sideline for wind sprints," Coach Cheesy announced. We did one after another until our tongues were hanging out of our mouths. They yelled at us to keep our feet moving. They really pushed us.

News of our lackadaisical effort reached the ears of Coach Jack. At our next practice, he took me aside and delivered a tough-love message.

"Eric, I've noticed in our games that you're not blocking out there, so we're not going to give you the ball until you start blocking," he declared. "I've seen you going through the motions. You're whiffing at guys. I can tell."

Until he said that, my attitude out there was the same as the one I had as a pitcher: *Coach, just give me the ball. Just give me the ball.* Didn't the results speak for themselves? I gained a lot of yards every game and scored a lot of touchdowns. We were winning nearly all our games. Wasn't that the point of playing?

But Coach Jack saw the bigger picture. I wasn't a team player and hadn't been for a few seasons. I wasn't blocking like I should, which meant I was letting my team down on plays when I *didn't* get the ball.

Here I thought I was the best player on the team and didn't have to listen to anybody, but that wasn't true at all. A bell went off in my head: *I'm gonna have to listen to these people. They are my coaches. I have to do what they say because I want to be a team player.*

I nodded to Coach Jack that I understood.

"Here's what we're going to do, young man," he said. "We're going to go back to basics and teach you how to block."

And that's what we did. I got a private tutorial in blocking, and we started from scratch. I had to learn to block all over again—and then block in our games and protect the quarterback from the pass rush. Even though I was following orders and blocking, it was still a couple of weeks before I started getting the ball again. But that only made me hungrier to play well.

———

I learned an invaluable lesson during my last season of Pop Warner— *Listen to your coaches.* Back in eighth grade, I didn't believe Coach Jack when he told me that if I didn't block, I wouldn't get the ball. I thought he wanted to win as badly as I did, and we both knew that our team had a better chance of victory when I ran the ball a lot. I thought Coach Jack would give me the ball because he liked me.

It turned out that Coach Jack disciplined me precisely *because* he did like me. Otherwise, he could have let me become a lazy blocker, someone who put myself before the team. If he had gone in that direction, I would have become an average player, all because of my lack of effort.

Thanks to him, I changed things around quickly. Boom! I started shoving bodies all over the place on the practice field, and those after-practice sprints—where I had mailed it in and didn't care if I came in last—turned into all-out bursts of pure speed from sideline to sideline. Sure, my lungs were about to burst and my legs felt like jelly, but I had to leave it all on the field.

Setting Sights High

I'm glad that Coach Jack, Coach Cheesy, and Coach Seaford didn't let me take the easy way out, and I owe them a lot. They were male role models at a time when I needed one.

The situation with my father was, well, complicated. We had a good relationship when he lived with Mom and me, but it was like this in our home: what my mom said is what went. My father was never much of a disciplinarian anyway.

I used to sleep downstairs with him when we moved into the new house in Avenel back when I was in kindergarten. But I was so young the day he came and told me that he was moving out and wouldn't be living with me any longer. "Okay, Dad," is all I could say. He said he was moving to Carteret, about three or four miles away. I didn't really understand what was going on. I was too young.

There was still some contact with my father after he left. He would take me fishing every now and then, but I never saw him at any of my football, basketball, or baseball games when I started elementary school. I just thought that was the way things were. When I was in middle school, though, he called my mother and asked her if she thought I would mind if he came to some of my games.

"Why don't you ask him?" Mom said.

So Dad called me up and said, "Would you mind if I came to watch you play?"

"No," I replied. "But you never came before. I thought you didn't care."

"I always cared about you, son, but I didn't think you'd want me showing up at your games."

"Yeah, you can come," I said. After that, I saw my father at nearly all my games—football, basketball, and baseball.

But because he didn't live with us, I basically adapted to my mom being both the mom and dad of the household, although I have to confess at that young age, I thought I should be the man of the house. I was a little tough guy, and that attitude carried out onto the football field before Coach Jack put me in my place.

During my final season of Pop Warner football, Mom gave me a set of weights for my birthday. They gathered dust throughout the fall, but after my attitude adjustment, I knew that I would have to work hard with those weights if I wanted to be an impact player in high school. I didn't know anything about how to go about that, however, so I asked my aunt's boyfriend, Ariel, if he would come up with a workout plan for me that I could start after my last Pop Warner game. Uncle Ariel—he's since married Auntie Cheryl—came up with a rigorous daily plan that would increase my muscle strength and give me some pop on the football field.

I made a commitment to myself that every single day I was going to work out to make myself a stronger and better football player. Then I asked my friend Nate Brown if he'd join me. Sure, he said, but he lasted only two weeks.

That was okay. Nothing was going to stop me—not even poor technique. I remember once when I was in the basement all by myself, the weighted bar got caught on my chest because I wasn't able to lift it anymore. I didn't have a spotter to help me out, so I had to figure out a way to get that bar off my chest. Mom was upstairs, but she had the TV on and couldn't hear me.

I tipped the weights one way, but that turned out to be the worst thing I could have done because everything became unbalanced. The heavy weights crashed to the floor.

My mom heard the ruckus and came running down the stairs. "What are you doing?"

I was in shock, lying there on the bench. "I'm sorry. I didn't mean to do that." I thought I had broken the whole house.

After that incident, I figured out a way to get the bar off my chest by rolling it all the way down my waist. When I learned to do that, I was not really afraid to lift by myself anymore. It was better when Nate came over and spotted me, but there were many times he didn't make it. I wasn't going to use the lack of a training partner as an excuse not to lift. I went from being barely able to lift anything to benching 185 pounds going into Colonia High School for my freshman year.

Heading into high school—the same one my mother, my sister, my aunt, and my uncle attended—was a big deal. Nothing was going to stop me from getting to where I wanted to go. By the time I started my freshman year, I had a favorite sport—football. Sure, I played baseball and basketball and liked those sports, too, but football gave me the biggest adrenaline high. Nailing a runner to the ground or running for a touchdown was awesome. No other sport could compare to the rush I received on the field.

When it came to playing football, I was all in from the top of my helmet to the cleats on my shoes.

THE UNEXPECTED CALL-UP

During the summer of 2004, I was gearing up for my first season of high school football, lifting weights with my teammates and organizing pickup games. We learned that the freshman team we hoped to join and rally behind was in jeopardy. We didn't have enough players to compete even though Colonia High was a large public school with 1,400 students and around three hundred and fifty incoming freshmen.

Only twenty kids came out for the first day of practice in August, two weeks before the start of school. We needed twenty-five players on the roster before we could take the field against other schools. Football wasn't an easy game, and kids my age knew it demanded a lot of effort and commitment, perhaps more than most were willing to give.

The coaching staff wasn't going to let something like poor turn-out get in our way, so they scrambled to find a half-dozen players. I'm not sure how they did it, but I didn't care. We had a team, and I was fired up to begin high school football. Six months of following Uncle Ariel's weight-training program had added new muscle to my frame. At the start of my freshman year, I was six feet, one inch tall and weighed just north of 200 pounds.

With such a small freshman squad, the coaches said I would be playing both ways: running back on offense and middle linebacker on defense. We had more than a few guys playing football for the first time, so on the first day of practice, Coach Ben LaSala gathered all the players—from the freshman, JV, and varsity teams—around him. "Take a seat, everyone!" Coach yelled out. Barrel-chested with a buzz cut and in his early forties, Coach LaSala had been the Colonia varsity football coach for the previous ten years, and his booming voice commanded respect.

"Gentlemen, I want you to find the warning sticker inside your helmet," he began.

I didn't know that football helmets came with warning stickers, but I found one attached to the plastic lining inside my helmet.

"Everyone find their sticker?" Coach LaSala asked. "Good. Let's read it out loud together."

In unison, here is what we read:

WARNING: Keep your head up. Do not butt, ram, spear, or strike an opponent with any part of this helmet or face guard. This is a violation of football rules and may cause you to suffer severe brain or neck injury, including paralysis or death and possible injury to your opponent. Contact in football may result in a concussion/brain injury, which no helmet can prevent. Symptoms include: loss of consciousness or memory, dizziness, headache, nausea, or confusion. If you have symptoms, immediately stop and report them to your coach, trainer, and parents. Do not return to a game or contact until all symptoms are gone and you receive medical clearance. Ignoring this warning may lead to another and more serious or fatal brain injury. NO HELMET SYSTEM

CAN PROTECT YOU FROM SERIOUS BRAIN AND/
OR NECK INJURIES, INCLUDING PARALYSIS OR
DEATH. TO AVOID THESE RISKS, DO NOT ENGAGE
IN THE SPORT OF FOOTBALL.

The warning was sobering. But Coach LaSala wasn't done yet.

"Listen up, men. You know football is a dangerous sport. You have to be a tough guy to play football. This is not a natural game. People aren't born to come out banging heads with each other. That's why you tackle with your shoulder. You don't lead with your head. Don't put your head down, because when you don't keep your head up, bad things can happen. When you tackle, I want you to tackle with your face up, not with your head down."

I had heard this type of speech before in Pop Warner, but it never hurt to have a refresher course. As we broke off to start our first drills of the season, Coach LaSala issued one more reminder to the team: "When you put your helmets on, strap them up and always keep your head up when you tackle."

Coach's words that day stayed with me for the rest of my football career. I understood the importance of keeping my chin up when making a tackle, but like any young teenager who thought he was invincible, I don't think it fully sunk in what a big risk I was taking by stepping onto a football field. All I knew at that time was that I loved the game, loved the contact, and loved winning.

I even enjoyed the tackling drills. I'd break down into the football position, where my feet were shoulder width and my knees were bent. Then I'd place my arms in the locked-and-loaded position with shoulders bent down, aiming at the target I wanted to hit.

If a runner came at me, I was taught to "bite the ball." I would put my face right on the ball as I wrapped up the player for the tackle. If I couldn't bite the ball, then I had to execute a "wrap and roll," grabbing the legs and rolling with it. If I couldn't wrap and roll, then the tackle of last resort was to dive for the runner or receiver's legs and try to trip him up by hitting his ankles.

I got pretty skilled at exploding at my target, putting my face right on the ball, and driving my adversary to the ground. Aggression was the key, and the more speed you had at the point of impact, the more likely you'd make a stop and plant the ballcarrier to the turf.

The Birthplace of College Football

I celebrated my fourteenth birthday on Saturday, September 4, 2004, by attending a big home game between Rutgers University and Michigan State. I knew all about Rutgers since the school was in my backyard—just twenty minutes away—and Mom had been a student there, although not for long.

Rutgers fans hadn't had much to cheer about for years. Head coach Greg Schiano (pronounced Shee-ah-no) was starting his third season at Rutgers, and the team hadn't finished above .500 in eleven seasons. Truth be known: Rutgers had some pitiful years (0–11, 1–10, 2–9, and 3–8) during that stretch, but the 2003 season was a ray of sunshine: Rutgers had gone 5–7, lifting everyone's hopes that Coach Schiano had turned around the oldest college program in the nation.

Rutgers was known as the Birthplace of College Football because the first-ever intercollegiate football game was played on November 6, 1869, on a plot of land where the Rutgers gymnasium sits today. Princeton was the foe, and Rutgers won 6–4. The Scarlet Knights, however, hadn't won many games since those post–Civil War days when football more resembled rugby since players didn't wear helmets of any kind. By the 1990s, when I was growing up, Rutgers had its hands full playing in the Big East conference against rivals like Syracuse, Pittsburgh, West Virginia, Louisville, Cincinnati, and South Florida.

On this particular day, Michigan State was in town for the first game of the season, and Rutgers fans set a stadium record with 42,612 in attendance. I went with Jack Nevins, my Pop Warner coach, and his sons John and Ray. Coach Jack and I shared the same birthday, and we all jumped for joy as the seconds ticked off a 19–14 win against a Big 10 opponent.

That day is truly when I came to love college football—the pageantry, the raucous student section, and the marching band music ringing loudly in my ears. The atmosphere was electric, and I wondered what it would be like to be one of those players. To run up and down that field, making plays—it seemed like the coolest thing ever.

While exiting the stadium, I ran into Coach LaSala, who was also at the game. "How about you come along for varsity practice on Monday," he asked me after wishing me a happy birthday. "You wanna do that?"

"Of course, Coach," I replied, my heart beating fast.

A freshman practicing—or possibly playing—with the varsity team was a big deal. Maybe Coach wanted to see if I could handle the next level. Maybe I was being called up.

I showed up for practice on Monday, not sure what was going to happen. Well, not very much did happen. The next day I was told to report for freshman team practice, with no explanation about why.

Back on the freshman team, we lost our first game to Monroe, but after that minor defeat, we couldn't be stopped, winning game after game, which certainly made it easier to suit up for practice each afternoon. I was a force at running back, and I made plenty of stops from my middle linebacker position. This was the first time I had ever played with guys my age, and I was enjoying myself because I was bigger and faster than my competition.

The freshman team was on a roll when Rob Starling, the starting middle linebacker on the varsity team, got injured. Coach LaSala didn't have a backup middle linebacker, so he said he was bringing me up from the freshman team for the last three games of the season.

I was surprised by Coach's decision; my "tryout" with the varsity earlier in the season had lasted only one day. We had no freshmen on the Colonia High varsity team—and only a handful in our league. But I had matured early, and I believed I had ability to compete at the varsity level. I was certainly ready to give it a good shot.

Even though I was eager to play, I was more nervous than ever. I had big shoes to fill. With only a few practices to learn our defense, the last thing I wanted to do was make a mistake and let my team down. In my first varsity game, I surprised myself—and my coaches—by making fifteen tackles on defense. Then I followed up that effort with seventeen tackles in the second game. Finally, I was good for thirteen tackles in the third and final game of the season.

In addition to being a terror on defense, I also played a little halfback and scored a touchdown in the last game of the season. This time, Mom couldn't run down the sideline as I strived for the goal line because she had to sit in the grandstands with her friends. I'm told, though, that she hollered and jumped up and down as I crossed the goal line. She and her friends exchanged congratulatory hugs.

But more than the nice stats I compiled, I truly had never played better in all three games. As the "quarterback" of the defense from my middle linebacker position, I was all over the field on every defensive play—pass or run. The coaches were amazed that I made so many clean tackles. Normally, ten tackles in a game is a lot. No one *averages* fifteen tackles a game.

I overheard Coach LaSala telling local reporters, "Where has this kid been all season? We could have won more games if we had LeGrand in our defensive backfield."

But Mom also heard that Coach LaSala was rather upset with his freshman team coaches for not telling him how much I had improved since my one-day tryout and that I was ready for varsity. Maybe it was because we were winning all our games and the frosh coaches didn't want the winning streak to end.

Throughout my three-week stint on the varsity team, I received a lot of back-slapping from Coach LaSala and his assistant coaches. When the season ended—we were a struggling team and even with my great tackles, we lost all three games—I immediately moved over to my next sport—basketball. Even though I was playing basketball and planned to get on the mound and play center field with the baseball team, I had a feeling that my future lay with football. And if that was going to be the case, I wanted to be the strongest and fastest player out there.

I resumed working out each evening with the weights in my basement. Uncle Ariel would often join me in those after-dinner workouts to spot and coach me with my lifting form. I was building myself into a powerful football player.

An Unexpected Pitch

As soon as the basketball season was over, it was baseball's turn. I played center field and pitched, just like in my Little League days. I could swing the bat, too: I had 47 home runs from ages eleven to thirteen, and I hit my share of dingers in freshman ball as well. I had grown to six feet, two inches, and I was in the 215-pound range. I was also a presence on the mound.

One of the great things about freshman baseball was that my varsity football coach, Ben LaSala, was also my baseball coach.

Coach was uptight and intense on the football field, where nothing got past his steely glare. But on a warm spring afternoon dressed in a baseball uniform, he was a jokester who loved hitting ground balls and pop flies during warm-ups and keeping things loose on the bench. We were one big, happy family, and I felt comfortable on the field because I knew a lot of the kids on the other teams from Woodbridge, Port Reading, and Sewaren. I had either played with them or against them in Little League and AAU ball. Now we were rivals.

I'll never forget one game against South River on a cold, drizzly spring day. I was on the mound, whipping the ball in there, but I was a little wild. Maybe I was really wild. Maybe I was so wild that I was hitting batters right and left. I pinged three pitches off the helmets of three different South River players. The second time they batted against me, they were too scared to stand in the batter's box, so they gave me half the plate. They didn't want to get plunked, which made my job easier.

Coach LaSala teased me the rest of the season for hitting those three batters. "Looks like you got all those little South River kids scared of you after hitting them in the head with that ninety-mile-an-hour fastball of yours."

"My bad, Coach. I'm sorry." I had a grin on my face.

I didn't know it at the time, but all of my weight lifting had started to bulk up my upper chest, and that altered my pitching motion. My body subtly made changes to the way I threw because of the new and bigger muscles on my frame. No wonder I had my wild days out there.

Unbeknownst to me during the baseball season, the Rutgers football team was recruiting Shamar Graves, a wide receiver from Woodbridge High, one of our main rivals. He was a junior, and many top college football programs try to lock up their blue-chip recruits at the end of their junior year by offering scholarships.

Shamar was rated as the No. 11 prospect in New Jersey high school football by Rivals.com, a network of websites that focus mainly on college football and basketball recruiting.

The Rutgers coaches were looking at film of Shamar playing against Colonia, and they kept seeing this kid flying around and making tackles.

"Who's that?" asked one coach.

"Some freshman that Bennie LaSala likes at Colonia. He's something, isn't he?"

That bit of film changed my life.

The story I heard was that after the Rutgers coaches saw me perform on five plays, they decided to offer me a scholarship.

To a freshman. With three games of varsity experience.

I know. It all sounds rather unbelievable, and it was.

Here's what happened: late in my freshman year, Mom was driving to work when her cell phone rang. Coach LaSala was on the phone.

"Are you sitting down?" he asked.

"Matter of fact, I'm in the car on my way to work," Mom said.

"Good, because I'm in the office with Joe Susan, one of the football coaches at Rutgers. He's here because he wants to offer Eric a full-ride scholarship."

Mom nearly drove off the road. The thought of not having to pay for my college education seemed preposterous to her. It was always going to be a tough road for a single mother, but now it looked like an open highway and college would be taken care of. I would have the chance to go to a university, get a degree, and gain a better start on life. Mom was practically hyperventilating. "I don't know what to say," my mother said, after she caught her breath.

"Listen, Karen, Coach Susan is not supposed to have any contact with Eric, because he's a freshman. Would you mind if I called Eric out of class to tell him myself?" Coach LaSala asked.

"Go ahead, Coach. I think he'll be thrilled."

I was in my Spanish I class when I got a message that Coach LaSala wanted to see me in his office. That was a strange request, especially coming in the morning.

I stepped into his office, and Coach LaSala asked me to close the door.

"Eric, Coach Joe Susan with the Rutgers football team drove over earlier this morning from New Brunswick because he wants to offer you a scholarship to play football at Rutgers."

My jaw dropped.

"I know you're just a freshman, but Coach Susan told me that you had made quite an impression on him and the Rutgers staff during your three games on varsity last season. He watched the film on you and said you were all over the place making tackles. He said he couldn't imagine where you're going to be when you're a senior."

This was all happening so fast, but Coach LaSala wasn't finished. "Coach Susan can't contact you directly because of NCAA recruiting rules, but he wanted me to remind you that Coach Schiano is turning the Rutgers football program around. Even though the team was 4–7 last year, the foundation has been laid for better things. Rutgers football wants you to be part of that turnaround. Even though it's only verbal at this time, that's why Rutgers is willing to offer you a full scholarship and have you come play for the Scarlet Knights."

My world spun. I was still a ninth grader, a lowly freshman. The only thing I could mumble was, "Really?"

Coach LaSala smiled. "Right now, Rutgers cannot formally offer you a scholarship in writing until your junior year. At that time, you can only make a verbal commitment until National Signing Day your senior year, which is always the first Wednesday in February. It's important that you continue to maintain good grades until then, so I'm sure you'll be motivated to pay attention in class and keep studying."

I was still stunned. *What? Is this really like a dream coming true? This fast after only three games?*

"Wow, thank you very much for telling me," I said. "I really appreciate it." I really didn't know what I could or should say.

Coach LaSala announced that the meeting was over. "Congratulations, Eric, but you got to get back to class. Float yourself back on a cloud if you want."

News Travels Quickly

After they shooed me out of the office, I was walking down the hall when I ran into a random guy, not even a close friend, and said, "Wow, Rutgers just offered me a scholarship to play football."

It didn't take long for the good news to blow through the school, and I heard that Coach LaSala was crazy with joy, telling all the faculty. Not many kids from Colonia High had ever gone on to play Division I football in the NCAA. The last player good enough was Piana Lukabu, who went to Rutgers in the early 2000s. A few had played at smaller programs, like Colgate and Harvard, but the general history was that one or two Colonia players every decade were good enough to play Division I football.

News of the Rutgers preemptive offer made its way around the recruiting circles. Within days, Al Golden, the defensive coordinator at the University of Virginia, called Coach LaSala and told him that he was upset that Virginia wasn't the first one to offer me a full ride. Other college football programs got wind of Rutgers's offer and said they wanted their chance as well.

We only had a week or two of baseball left, but after the

thunderbolt from Rutgers, my heart wasn't in baseball anymore. It was nice to finish with a winning season as we compiled a 17–10 record, but after the last out was recorded, I knew I was hanging up my mitt for good. I was done with baseball and done with basketball.

From then on, football would become my life, and I would do whatever it took to make myself a better player. All I wanted to do was lift, work out, and get stronger.

Money was tight in our household, and I knew Mom always regretted not finishing college, so she was constantly talking to me about the value of earning a degree and getting a good job. If football could pay for college, then I would get that degree for sure.

I lifted with my team all that summer in our weight room at Colonia High. I needed the camaraderie and accountability that came with lifting with my teammates. I liked the social part of lifting together, hanging out with Nate Brown, Ryan Don Diego, Ray and John Nevins, and our new teammate, Joey LaSala. This was a time to bond. To work toward a common goal. To take some responsibility. I was growing up and becoming a man.

I was bulking up, transforming into the build of a football player. By the end of the summer, I could clean-and-jerk 225 pounds, and on the bench, I improved from 185 pounds to 275 pounds. Coach LaSala told the local newspaper that I was a "freak of nature, a big-time player."

Each summer, nearly every Division I school holds a summer camp for high school players, which is a good way to improve your football skills but also a good way to showcase your abilities. The summer between my freshman and sophomore years, I attended the Rutgers summer football camp, where I met Coach Schiano for the first time and was greatly impressed with his energy and leadership. During the four-day camp, the players were separated into position groups to work with the position coaches. This was not a full-contact camp—players weren't even allowed to bring helmets. We ran through drills—mine were for running back and linebacker positions—and seven-on-seven scrimmages in T-shirts, shorts, and football cleats.

Every now and then, one of the position coaches would pull me off to the side for a talk. It wasn't so much about what was happening on the field but *How are you doing?* and *Are you liking it here?*—stuff like that. That's how the recruiting process works, getting players familiar with the school's way and forming relationships. You get a look at them, and they get a look at you.

For many of the players like myself, this was our first time in a college setting. We stayed in the athletic dorm, where the nights got pretty crazy with a lot of fooling around. There were kids running around and throwing baby powder on other people's doors or tossing water balloons around the halls. We were having tons of fun being on our own. I wasn't homesick at all.

Coach LaSala's son, Joe, who was the same year as me at neighboring South River High School, was at camp too. A week into camp, Joe told my teammate Nate Brown and me that he was transferring to Colonia in the fall so he could join our team and be coached by his father. He wanted to keep the news on the down low, so no one knew—or was supposed to know.

One night, our Colonia crew was hanging out in the commons with the South River crew, and Nate said in front of everybody, "So, Joey, I hear you're transferring to Colonia next year."

Immediate silence. And then Joe, with the straightest face ever, said, "I don't know what you're talking about."

I punched Nate in the shoulder and told him to shut up. But now the word was out thanks to Nate's loose lips, and there was nothing we could do about it.

Two months later, Joe and his family moved into our school district, and Joe played wide receiver on our team. Today, Joey LaSala is one of my very best friends.

When I came home from the Rutgers camp, I felt like I had a track to follow. I knew I was bettering myself each and every day and couldn't wait for the football season to start. I was getting stronger and bigger than my friends and teammates. I could feel it in the work ethic that I was developing, and I could envision the payoff somewhere down the line for a game you play ten times a year.

I was ready to make my mark in varsity football.

THE LETTERS NEVER STOP

During the summer before my sophomore year, Mom and I were having dinner at home when she became awfully quiet.

"Eric, you know that I've always been very open with you."

Mom was always one to speak her mind when the occasion warranted it, but I had a feeling that this time she didn't want to talk about football.

I was right. She wanted to talk about sex.

"You're fourteen, soon to be fifteen, so you're coming into a time of your life when you'll have certain feelings. I was wondering if you knew about sex."

Man, this was embarrassing. "I know all about it, Mom. We learned about this in health."

"Good, but maybe they didn't tell you everything. Or maybe they didn't tell you that you aren't ready yet. Did they talk to you about AIDS?"

I rolled my eyes. "Yes, they talked to us about AIDS."

"Well, AIDS is a really scary disease, and if you have sex, you could get AIDS, and if you get AIDS, you'll die."

Yes, Mom was trying to scare me. She knew that you don't automatically get AIDS if you have sex and that you don't automatically die because you get AIDS, but she was trying to make a big impression on me—to wait.

"There are different types of girls out there, so I don't want you to be influenced by fast girls," she said. "They are the ones who will get you into trouble. So you have to be smart, and you have to be respectful. You don't do something just to do it. This is not the time to rush into anything because no kid is ready to have sex at age fourteen."

I squirmed in my seat. This was the most embarrassing conversation ever, but that was typical Mom looking out for me. She had always been open, even blunt. She always said we could talk about anything, but being a teen boy, I didn't exactly want to talk to Mom about girls and all that. So she didn't wait for me to bring up the subject, because she knew I wouldn't. What she wanted to do that evening was to get the point across that feelings for girls were normal, that I wasn't ready yet, and neither were the girls. So wait.

What I wasn't willing to wait for was my first full season of varsity football to start. Once again, on the first day of August practice, Coach LaSala gathered us around for an important announcement. "Gentlemen, take off your helmets and look at what the warning sticker says inside." Then Coach asked us to read the warning label all together out loud, which we did.

WARNING: Keep your head up. Do not butt, ram, spear, or strike an opponent with any part of this helmet or . . .

"Very good, guys," Coach LaSala said when we were done. "The reason why I have you guys read the warning label every year is because it's super important. You have to keep your head up when you tackle. Bad things happen when you lead with the head, so don't use your helmet as a battering ram. You'll get hurt, perhaps severely injured. Instead, remember to 'bite the ball' and play solid, hard-nosed football the Patriot way."

He was right about the hard-nosed football part. I was on the receiving end of one of those hits during a game against Carteret High when I gathered in a screen pass. I thought I had a couple of linemen out in the flat with me, but I guess I didn't because their strong-side defensive end Jason Adjepong Worilds leveled me with a thundering shot that nailed me to the ground like a stake. I was shook up pretty bad and had no idea what was going on after that collision. (Jason was an All-Stater who went on to Virginia Tech and wound up being a second-round draft pick with the Pittsburgh Steelers in 2010, where he's now part of the Steel Curtain defense. Good luck, NFL.)

Most of the time, though, I was making good yardage with the ball in my hands and delivering my own Worilds-like shots from the linebacker position. I was more than holding my own out there on the field. My coaches were pleased with how I was playing and decided to move me from fullback (the guy who usually blocks) to halfback (the guy who's getting the handoff from the quarterback and expected to churn out big yards to keep the offense moving).

I had some big games, like against South Plainfield when I ran for 216 yards on thirty-six carries—a six-yards-per-carry average—to help us win our first game of the season. I also recorded eleven tackles, including a "signature hit"—which is how the local newspaper described my body slam on running back Jamar Beverly. It was sure better pile-driving a runner to the ground than being on the receiving end.

Coach LaSala sang my praises to any reporter who would listen. "Eric is unbelievable," he told one local newspaper. "He's the best fifteen-year-old I've ever seen. He won't outrun you, but he'll barrel over you. We recently moved Eric to halfback. We're not going to be fancy anymore. We're just going to give him the ball. Eric is a big-time player. If there's someone out there better than him at his age, I'd like to see him."

Letters Filling the Mailbox

Because of my strong play, recruiting letters started flowing into our Avenel mailbox from dozens of college football programs. Big-name programs like Notre Dame, the Big 10 schools like Michigan, Michigan State, and Ohio State; the Southeastern Conference schools like Alabama, Florida, and Tennessee; and every Big East school that played in Rutgers's conference were flooding my mailbox with letters and slick promotional material.

There were days when I received fifteen letters or brochures. It was ridiculous. Some programs sent me a letter every day for a week or two at a time. (I guess that's nothing: Alvin Kamara, a tailback from Georgia scheduled to graduate from high school in 2013, received 105 letters from the University of Alabama in *one day!*)

Many of these letters were variations of the same theme:

Dear Eric:

I want to take this opportunity to tell you how much we are interested in having you come play for State U to further your education after you graduate from high school. We think you'd be a fine addition to the fine group of young men enrolling with your class, and we know you'd be a proud member of the class of '12 at State U. The football staff believes that with young men of your caliber, we all will be able to look forward to a great future. We are confident that you will do well at State U, both in the classroom and on the playing field.

We want to wish you the best of luck during the rest of your high school athletic career. We know that you will do well. The whole staff joins me in urging you to put forth a concentrated effort on your scholastic work as well over the next three years. The academic background you have when you arrive at State U will go a long way in determining your success during your college football career.

Again, my staff and I will continue to follow your progress and would love to have you visit our beautiful campus during one of our home games. If that sounds like something you'd like to explore, please contact my personal assistant so that we can arrange a visit.

Until then, I send you my highest regards.

(Signed)
Coach Big Name

I didn't open every letter, especially those from schools that sent me two, three, four, or sometimes five pieces of mail each week. It wasn't that I was ungrateful, but I didn't have time with school, practice, homework, and playing games.

We had a so-so year my sophomore season, finishing 5–5, which qualified us for the state playoffs and a matchup against Middletown South, the No. 1 seed in the state playoffs for our division. They were huge. They were gigantic. They had three players who went on to Division I programs at Stanford, Georgia, and Lehigh. We got destroyed, 52–26, and it could have been worse.

In terms of stats, though, I had a great year: 1,064 yards rushing (or a little more than 100 yards per game) and 109 tackles (or a little more than ten per game). I also ran my fastest 40-yard dash ever—a 4.71. That's about where you want to be to chase down quick running backs. For the rest of my football career, I'd be in the

4.7s, which is excellent for a linebacker but a little slow for what coaches want to see out of their running backs.

Even though I could be a dominant halfback at the high school level, I knew my future was on the defensive side of the ball in college football. Something about chasing down a runner and stopping him cold gave me a bigger adrenaline rush than playing running back. Even during my first season of varsity football, I put a lot more passion into defense than the "glory role" of running back.

When the season was over, I still headed over to the Colonia High gym every day to continue my weight training. I was really starting to increase the weight I lifted, so much so that Coach Collins used to bark at me for bending the bars in the weight room and having to buy new ones. I was up to 335 pounds on the squat—fifty pounds more since the summer. I was motivated to work hard during the off-season. Getting stronger and faster was the only way to prepare for playing time on a Division 1 team.

When the sophomore year ended, I participated in my second Rutgers summer football camp and brought several teammates with me. Three dozen other colleges wanted me to come to their summer camp. Summer camps are an important part of the recruitment process between the sophomore and junior years. The upcoming junior year is when the college football coaches put a full-court press on you to come to their school.

But I passed on all the other college football camps for two reasons:

1. They were all out of town, and Mom didn't have the money to pay for the airfare.
2. I was happy with Rutgers. They treated me like family. Besides, Coach Joe Susan told me at the Rutgers summer camp that he couldn't wait to put his scholarship offer in writing on September 1, 2006, the start of my junior year of high school.

True to what Coach Susan said to Coach LaSala's at the end of my freshman year, Rutgers *did* offer me a full-ride football scholarship at the start of my junior year, just as promised.

Sure, it was a piece of paper, but Rutgers's scholarship offer in writing represented a lot more to me—a momentous opportunity to have my college education paid for and to play football on a big stage.

Pandemonium in Piscataway

At the start of my junior season in 2006, things were really looking up at Rutgers. Coach Schiano had guided the Scarlet Knights to their first winning season in fourteen years in 2005 and only the second bowl game in Rutgers's 136-year history of playing football. Rutgers fans, long dormant, were jumping on the bandwagon again.

The scholarship offer from Rutgers was certainly greeted with enthusiasm by Mom and me, but we were not ready to give our verbal agreement during my junior season. Too many other teams wanted me to play for them, so we thought we'd let things settle a bit and see what developed.

But then Rutgers kept winning. And winning. And winning. Going into the ninth game of the season, the Scarlet Knights were *undefeated* at 8–0, and next up was a home game against the Louisville Cardinals, who were the No. 3 team in the country at 7–1 and coming off a big victory over highly regarded West Virginia.

I just *had* to be there at Rutgers Stadium with my buddies, and I'm sure glad I went. It was a great game played on a Thursday night before a national audience looking in on ESPN. It was anyone's game up until Jeremy Ito kicked a tie-breaking 28-yard field goal with thirteen seconds left to give Rutgers a 28–25 lead.

When Derain Thompson sacked Louisville quarterback Brian

Brohm on the last play of the game, I was among the tens of thousands of crazy fans who stormed the field to celebrate. "It's pandemonium in Piscataway," exclaimed Rutgers Radio play-by-play announcer Chris Carlin while I danced on the field with my buddies and slapped the shoulder pads of the victors. (A little geography lesson: Rutgers Stadium in located in Piscataway, while most of the Rutgers campus is situated in New Brunswick.) In the happiness of that cool evening, I imagined that one day I, too, would be part of an awesome scene like this.

The mantra of the Rutgers team was "Keep Chopping!" Coach Schiano, while prowling the sidelines, would frequently slam the edge of his right hand into the palm of his left in a chopping motion. He wanted the players to imagine that they were in a forest all by themselves, but they each had an axe in their hands. "You take your time chopping down one tree," Coach Schiano said, "and when that tree falls, you take a breath and then you go on to the next one. Football is just like that. It doesn't matter whether you're on offense, defense, or special teams, you keep chopping, taking each play one at a time. When you win that battle, you go on to the next. You chop, chop, chop all game long, and eventually you'll come out of the forest with a victory."

"Keep chopping!" was a great motivational metaphor that tapped into the ebb and flow of football games: you have to keep plugging away, never giving up. Since victory often doesn't come until the very end in football, at least not until the last seconds tick off, you have to continue "chopping" until success is assured.

The Rutgers players were getting into this chopping thing, especially after defensive tackle Eric Foster was caught by TV cameras "chopping" after big plays. I started doing my own chopping at Colonia High, and any college football coach closely watching game film from my junior year would have noticed that after a big stop, I'd often get up from the pile and make a quick chopping motion with my right hand into the palm of my left. I had to be careful how demonstrative I could be, though, since I didn't want to get an "excessive celebration" flag thrown by the refs.

Unfortunately, Colonia High wasn't experiencing the same level of success as Rutgers. We started the season with high hopes, and I was amazed when Coach LaSala made me a team captain as a junior—the first time that had ever happened in Colonia High history. Coach LaSala, who felt like I was showing the leadership qualities that merited being named a team captain as an underclassman, loved talking me up with the press. "Eric's the best I've ever coached," he said early in the season. "It's not so much how dominating he is, but the fact that he didn't turn sixteen until September 4 is scary. The kid bench-presses three hundred and fifty pounds, which is unheard of."

I tried not to get a big head after hearing that. "I read the stuff about me, but it doesn't faze me," I told John Haley with the *Home News Tribune*. "My mother raised me to be level-headed, plus my coaches from Pop Warner to high school have had a big influence on me and keep me on the right track. There are some people who think I'm overrated, too, so that motivates me to play well."

Even though my teammates and I had all the motivation in the world, we finished my junior season with a 3–7 record, which was a huge disappointment. But personally I had my biggest year as a linebacker with 150 tackles, or fifteen per game, so the cards and letters kept arriving in our mailbox each day. Dozens of schools wanted me to visit on official recruiting trips.

Even though I was loyal to Rutgers, Mom and I decided that I should look at some out-of-state schools just to be sure. I took recruiting trips to the University of Maryland, the University of Virginia, and the University of Notre Dame during and after my junior season. I made plans to visit the University of Florida, Florida State University, and the University of Miami in the fall of my senior year—all great schools with great football programs. The Miami Hurricanes were my favorite college team growing up because I used to choose the 'Canes as my team whenever I played the *NCAA Football* video game on my PlayStation.

What was I looking for in a school? For starters, I wanted an excellent education, but I was also looking for a great family atmosphere with the coaches and the football program. I wanted to attend a school where I could develop my skills as a football player. After that, it was a matter of weighing the intangibles, like the distance from home or the academic program in place for the football players.

During my visit to the University of Maryland, I met Vernon Davis, a 254-pound tight end. He was a ripped guy with a set of ridiculous washboard abs. I heard other recruits wonder, "If we come here, will we look like him?"

I enjoyed my visit to the University of Virginia. The campus had a lot of charm, but the South was not for me—just a bit too country. My official recruiting visit to Notre Dame was a broadening experience as well, but the school felt too far from home for me.

Each school I visited had its own characteristics—and its own pluses and minuses. The trick was finding the school that best matched my needs and my desires.

As it turned out, though, the choice wasn't completely up to me: I also needed to prove myself academically before I'd get my chance to play.

The Dreaded SAT

All the full-ride scholarship offers I received from these great schools had one contingency attached to them: I had to score at least a 910 on my SATs. That seemed quite doable. I had always been a "good" student even though I had been diagnosed with ADHD—attention deficit/hyperactivity disorder—back in second grade.

My grades were adequate at Colonia: lots of B's and C's. But sitting in a chair for three hours on a Saturday morning for an SAT test wasn't my strong suit. I was not a great standardized-test taker or even a good one.

When I sat for my first SAT test midway through my junior year, I was nervous. The motivation to do well was there. I concentrated hard for nearly four hours, and when the test was over, I set my No. 2 lead pencil down. I hoped I had done well enough.

When the results came back, I learned that I had received a score of 1060. I made it! Ten-sixty is better than 910, right?

I texted Coach Urban Meyer at the University of Florida—the Gators wanted me, too—with the good news. I texted Charlie Weis at Notre Dame and a bunch of other schools telling them that I qualified academically. I received replies congratulating me and saying they'd be faxing me a scholarship offer in the morning.

Then Coach LaSala got wind of what I had done and called me into his office. "Eric, you didn't make it," he announced. "You got a 790 on the first two parts, Mathematics and Critical Reading. The 1060 was for all three parts, including the Writing section."

Ooh. That wasn't good news.

"But Coach, I just texted all those coaches that I'm qualified. And now . . ."

"Don't worry about it. I'll handle everything. Bottom line is you didn't make it, so we'll have to keep working at it."

I was devastated by this news. *Are you kidding me? Can I be that dumb?*

Maybe I had a bad day. I signed up for the next SAT, but I showed only a slight improvement, moving the bar from 790 to 830. Then I tried the ACT test, but that was a disaster, too.

We had a major problem on our hands. My scholarship offers

and dreams of playing college football at a four-year school were ruined if I didn't get my SAT score up. With an 830, I wasn't going anywhere except a junior college.

Coach LaSala recommended that we bite the bullet and put me in a SAT tutor program. Mom called around, didn't like the vibes from several learning centers, but she clicked with the person at Princeton Review, which had a program where they would send a tutor to our house. It was a bit more expensive this way, but Mom thought I'd do better in a one-on-one setting rather than a class atmosphere.

The cost: $2,800.

This was a lot of money for us. I tried to tell her it was too much to pay, that I'd do better next time, that I'd try my hardest, but she was insistent, saying that if $2,800 got my college education paid for, then it would all be worth it. She put the large fee on her credit card, and off we went.

My tutor was awesome. She came twice a week to my house after school and worked with me for two months during the spring of my junior year.

My next SAT was scheduled for April. I was prepared for the battle. When Mom dropped me off, she looked me in the eyes. "Oh, God, good luck," she said.

I needed the prayer.

Two weeks later, I received my test results at school, and the numbers set off some whooping and hollering in the hallways. I got an 1190 on Mathematics and Critical Reading, an increase of 400 points or 50 percent, from my first attempt, and a 1650 on all three SAT tests!

"Maybe I should go to Harvard," I joked to Mom.

This time, I didn't text any college coaches, but I did text Coach LaSala, and he replied: "Amazing! This is great news!"

It really was.

Recruiting Visitors

As word got out that I was eligible for a scholarship, coaches from more and more programs came to Colonia High to visit me. It felt like every other day I was getting called out of class.

I was on my way back from a bathroom break from chemistry class one morning—well, a prolonged bathroom break that included a long, long stop to sample some of the fresh chocolate chip cookies from the cooking class—when I saw my chemistry teacher running after me. "Eric, you have to get to the Guidance Office now! A coach from Penn State is waiting for you there."

I did a U-turn and sprinted to the Guidance Office, where a perturbed Coach LaSala was cooling his heels. He got in my face and said, "I'm going to jack you up!"

Wondering what I had done wrong, I backed up to the wall as he advanced on me.

"Where have you been?" he demanded. "I had half my health class looking for you."

"I was in the Cooking Room, Coach."

"What were you doing in the Cooking Room? You were supposed to be in—"

A smile formed on Coach LaSala's lips. "Oh, I know. Making sure the cookies weren't poisoned, right?"

I looked around the Guidance Room, and the other counselors had their heads down. Coach LaSala calmed down and led me to a nearby conference room, where a Penn State football coach had been waiting patiently to see me. He had been told that I was home sick and was on my way to see him, which is why I was delayed.

I survived that morning even though I thought Coach was going to kill me. But I almost didn't survive the glare I received from Charlie Weis, head coach of Notre Dame, when he dropped by Colonia High to talk to Coach LaSala about me.

"Coach Weis was very specific," Coach LaSala told me before his arrival. "He said he didn't want anything crazy going on when he gets here."

"Got it," I replied.

Coach's smartphone buzzed. "I'm here" was the message from Coach Weis.

A long, sleek black limousine with tinted windows rolled up to the school entrance.

Coach was approaching the car when two students rushed up to him, clutching pieces of paper. "Can we have your autograph?" one of them said as Coach Weis stepped out of the limo. I guess word got around that he was visiting.

More students started to head over, but Coach LaSala shooed them away. Our principal was waiting inside, and the next thing you know, pictures were being taken of Coach LaSala, our principal, and Charlie Weis seated at the table, with Coach Weis's huge Super Bowl ring clearly visible on his right hand. He had won four of them over the years coaching for the New York Giants and New England Patriots.

Apparently, this was an "unofficial visit," so Coach Weis had to "talk" to me through my coach. So he'd look at Coach LaSala and say things like:

I think Eric would really like coming to Notre Dame.

Tell Eric that our recruiting class is rated in the top ten.

Rules are rules, and rule compliance was a big deal with college football coaches.

Decision Time

What I was learning through this process was that the top football schools all wanted to know where they stood by the end of your junior year, so they press recruits to make a commitment, one way or another, before the start of summer camps.

Late one afternoon in May, I received a phone call from Coach Schiano. We made the usual small talk, and then he got down to business.

"Eric, we have been recruiting you since your freshman year, and we have been by your side through everything. We really want you to come and play here at Rutgers. We had a big season last year. We were 11–2 and ranked number twelve in the nation. We want you to come be a part of the excitement at Scarlet Nation, so now we need to know where your head is at. Have you made a decision? Can we count on you coming to Rutgers in the summer of 2007?"

I needed to scramble out of the pocket. "Coach, can I call you back?"

He said that was fine, and Coach reminded me that he was available for any questions I might have.

I hung up and thought about how Rutgers had been with me through this whole recruiting thing. They were always my number one. They offered me as a freshman, they were close to home, and I had been on campus a hundred times. There was a family atmosphere, and I believed that Coach Schiano and his assistants honestly cared about me as a person and as a football player.

I called Mom and told her about the phone call from Coach Schiano. We knew this call was coming sooner or later, and now it looked like things were coming to a head. "Mom, I'm thinking about committing myself to Rutgers."

"Are you sure?" she asked. "Is this really where you want to go?" Mom was asking me to think this through one more time because this decision would impact my future in many different ways. She knew I was only sixteen years old and wouldn't be seventeen until the following September, so I didn't have a lot of experience with life-changing choices such as the one before me.

I exhaled a deep breath. "I believe Rutgers is where I want to go. You can go to all my home games, and I'd be close to home. They've recruited me from day one."

I could hear my mother relax on the other side of the phone. "If you want to go to Rutgers, I'll be more than happy," she said.

"Good. Let me call Coach Schiano back."

Just five minutes had passed when I reached Coach Schiano. I didn't waste any time. "Coach, I've made my decision. I'm coming to Rutgers."

Once again, I heard an adult say, "Are you sure?"

"Yes, I'm sure."

There was a pause. "So you're telling me that you're giving me your word. Only men give their word and really mean it and keep it."

"Coach, I'm giving you my word. I know I might be a young man, but I'm giving you my word that I'm coming to Rutgers. And I'm not changing my mind."

I heard another exhale of relief on the line. "Eric LeGrand, let me be the first to welcome you to Rutgers University. Congratulations. You are now part of the Rutgers football family."

Then Coach put his phone on speaker, and it was apparent that he was in his office or a conference room because several Rutgers coaches hollered their congratulations. That just confirmed in my heart that I had made the right choice.

The next phone call Coach Schiano made was to Coach La-Sala to tell him the good news. "I don't want Eric to see any more coaches because he's committed to us," Coach Schiano said.

Over the next few weeks, and right through my senior season, coaches from Virginia, Michigan, and Michigan State contacted Coach LaSala to make their pitch with me, but he said I had committed to Rutgers and that decision was firm. I was so gung-ho for Rutgers that I started recruiting *my* friends—the ones I had met at the Rutgers summer camps—to come join me at Piscataway. I got Scott Vallone from Long Island and Art Forst from Manasquan, New Jersey, to commit. It was shaping up to be a great freshman class at Rutgers, but I still had some unfinished business at Colonia High.

Finishing Strong

I dropped down to 240 pounds for my senior year, ten fewer than my junior weight, because I felt that 250 was too heavy to be playing linebacker even though I made a bunch of tackles during my junior season. It wasn't a lack of discipline that got me up to 250, although I was basically eating everything I wanted to. Our coaches were on all of us to add weight, so I went with the program. In fact, there were times I tipped the scales at 260 pounds during my junior year. But I worked hard during the off-season—and laid off Mom's fresh-baked chocolate chip cookies—to slim down to 240 pounds for my final year of high school football.

We also had an excellent turnaround on the field, winning seven of ten games and capturing our first Greater Middlesex Conference White Division championship since 1999. You could tell Rutgers was on my mind when we defeated a tough South Plainfield team in double overtime, 10–7. "We just kept coming back, kept chopping the whole game," I told a reporter from the Newark-based *Star-Ledger*. I'm sure Coach Schiano was smiling when he read that. Our conference championships qualified us for the state championship playoffs with a first-round matchup against Scotch Plains–Fanwood High School. We felt this was our year.

Before the game, Coach LaSala pulled me aside. "I've got good news and bad news," he said. "The bad news is Jordan Edmonds can't start. The good news is that you know all the plays, so you're going to play quarterback tonight."

I gulped. I knew that our quarterback hadn't been feeling well all week, and during the pregame meal, Jordan sipped Pepto-Bismol instead of eating with the rest of the team. But I had all the confidence in the world that I could quarterback this team to victory.

First down on offense, I dropped back and hit my friend Nate Brown on a post route, good for twelve yards. Then I had to roll out to escape a blitz. As I headed toward the sideline, looking for an open receiver, the ball fell out of my hand. I watched helplessly as it bounced out of bounds, allowing us to retain possession.

On my next pass, I was going long the entire way. I saw Cory Jacik streaking up the sideline. It looked like he had a step or two on his man, so I chucked the ball up there, sixty yards in the air. I must have put too much oomph under the throw because their cornerback intercepted the ball. Maybe playing quarterback wasn't as easy as I thought.

After three series, Coach LaSala had seen enough. He inserted a pale-looking Jordan Edmonds back into the game, and he threw five interceptions. In all, we had eight turnovers and lost by six points, 19–13.

I was devastated. We should have easily won that game. I felt like we were definitely the better team, but the turnovers killed us. After the final seconds ticked off, I sat on the ground and couldn't stop my body from shaking uncontrollably. I felt responsible for the loss, I had let my team down, shattering our state championship dreams.

Coach LaSala did a great job of keeping our spirits high after the letdown against Scotch Plains–Fanwood. We still had one more game left—our annual rivalry game against Woodbridge High, which was always played the Saturday after Thanksgiving. We dressed in our locker room at Colonia for the Saturday morning game before boarding a bus for the ride over to Woodbridge. As a senior, I knew this was it—my last game in a high school uniform. We were playing for the Bragging Rights trophy against our cross-town rivals, so this was our chance to finish strong.

Leaving the locker room, I passed under the door, where a sign was attached just above the transom. In big black block letters, it said:

BELIEVE

My teammates jumped and tapped that sign as they exited the locker room, a ritual that bonded us together before every game. *Believe* was our motto. We had to *believe* that we would play well and win. There was power in the conviction of things not yet seen.

For the last time as a Colonia High football player, I jumped and tapped the sign with my left hand, slapping my fingers on the EL . . . for my initials, Eric LeGrand.

We won my final game of high school football against Wood-bridge High, but little did I know that **BELIEVE** would come to mean something completely different for me at Rutgers University.

6

NEW BEGINNING IN NEW BRUNSWICK

After I signed my National Letter of Intent in early February, I asked Coach Schiano if I could work out at the Hale Center on the Rutgers campus every day after school. I wanted to keep in shape for my first season of college football. I could, he replied, as long as I did my own weight-training program and didn't have any contact with the team or any of the coaches.

I was impressed by the Football Team Room, which was the home of the Scarlet Knights' training, administrative, and academic resource facilities. The shiny place was state-of-the-art, complete with a game room featuring plush leather couches, flat-screen TVs, and pool tables. The massive and well-appointed weight room wasn't shabby, either.

My school day was over at 11 A.M. my senior year, so I worked out a routine with my grandmother and mother so I could lift at Rutgers. Nana would pick me up from school and hand me two turkey burgers on wheat bread, which I would eat on our way to nearby Clark, where Mom worked. I was watching what I ate because I wanted to drop ten pounds and get down to 230 pounds—a good weight for a linebacker. Since I didn't have my own wheels—we couldn't afford a second car—I picked up Mom's well-used 1996 Honda Accord by her office and drove it to Rutgers, where I worked out during the afternoon, returning in time to pick her up as she got off work.

With such a busy schedule, the rest of my senior year passed quickly, right up until prom. I had a long-distance girlfriend, but she lived in Chicago and couldn't come to the prom, so I asked my best friend, Brandon Hall, if he knew anyone. He talked to his prom date, and she said she had a friend who would love to go with me. On the morning of the prom, however, she learned her uncle had died in Florida. She had to get on a plane to Miami right away. There I was, three or four hours before my senior prom, with no date.

My friend Ray Nevins knew someone who might be available. When he called, she was not only free, but she had a formal dress in her closet ready to go. There was one snag, though—she attended Woodbridge High, our biggest rival. But with just a few hours to go before the dance, I wasn't ready to let a little school rivalry get in the way of having a great night at prom with my friends.

I entered the Marriott hotel ballroom in Bridgewater with my date, Nicole Caggiano, on my arm and stares from my friends. *Who's that good-looking girl with EL?* Nicole turned out to be the best prom date ever. She was an All-State bowler who hit if off quickly with my friends, and they talked about friends they had in common. What could have been an awkward evening wasn't awkward at all.

My days at Colonia were quickly coming to an end. Within weeks of senior prom, I was enrolled at Rutgers. (Because the Rutgers football program expected all players to attend summer school and participate in preseason weight training, I had to report at

Rutgers on Tuesday, June 24, 2008.) Colonia High, however, was holding their commencement exercises two days later! This meant, technically speaking, that I attended Rutgers University without a high school diploma for forty-eight hours.

I'll admit that I felt a little grown-up, being a "college student" while I walked with Colonia High's Class of 2008, wearing my cobalt-blue graduation gown. When I saw Mom beaming in the bleachers as I walked to receive my diploma, I was pumped. I knew a bright future awaited me at Rutgers. While it was sad to say good-bye to my high school friends and teammates, I knew I'd stay in touch with many of them. I was hoping they'd come to my games at Rutgers Stadium.

After tossing our mortarboards into the air, our class celebrated Grad Night at a rec center where there was basketball and Ping-Pong, palm reading by a psychic, and even back massages from therapists. The idea was to provide an alternative to a night of drinking.

Not that I was planning on boozing it up for Grad Night. I wasn't much of a partier during high school. Sure, I had a beer or two every now and then, but I didn't drink much because I was focused on playing football at a Division I school. As for marijuana and other drugs, I never smoked in my life—cigarettes, weed, none of that. I was just never interested.

Mom was pretty strict about partying. If I heard it once, I heard it a hundred times from her: "Nothing good happens after midnight." She gave me a midnight curfew on weekends, even though some of my friends didn't have to be home at any certain time. I'm sure the early morning accident that claimed the life of Uncle Jimmy weighed on her mind.

But now that I was going off to college and living on my own for the first time, I had no curfew. I was excited for the freedom, but I was also nervous because I wanted to meet the expectations of Coach Schiano and his staff as well as Mom and my family.

New Position

I adapted well to the new routine of college. Mom wasn't emotional at all when I left home, because I was so close and came home every weekend.

During the week, I lived with the Rutgers football team in Metzger Hall, a four-story redbrick dorm on Busch Campus with eighteen-foot-by-twelve-foot rooms. Metzger is where the athletic department housed athletes from various sports during the summer "bridge" program, which was mandatory for football players as well as the young men and women playing on the basketball teams. I had a great summer getting to know the guys on the football team before training camp started in early August.

Life was fairly simple. I would wake up, have breakfast, attend a writing class, and then work out at the Hale Center. Many afternoons, the players would arrange games called "seven-on-sevens," which are T-shirt-and-shorts, no-contact scrimmages involving seven offensive players against seven defensive players. Since I was going to be a linebacker at Rutgers, I ran around covering running backs coming out of the backfield.

The seven-on-sevens were student-run because NCAA rules forbid coaches from participating in any preseason workouts until the start of training camp. When training camp finally opened the first week of August, I stopped by the equipment room to pick up my gear and choose a jersey number. At Colonia High, I had worn number 30 because Terrell Davis, a running back for the Denver Broncos back in my Pop Warner days, played with 30 across his orange jersey. I loved the way TD ran the ball, and he was my favorite player when I was growing up. In fact, the Broncos were my favorite NFL team, even though the New York Jets and New York Giants played in my backyard.

In college and pro football, though, 30 wasn't a linebacker number, so I chose number 52 because I was a huge fan of Ray Lewis, the ferocious middle linebacker for the Baltimore Ravens who was a Pro Bowl lock every year. The dude was the best sideline-to-sideline player in football. He always got his man.

I was putting away my new jerseys and equipment when Bob Fraser, the linebackers coach, approached me shortly after check-in. "Coach wants to see you in his office," he said.

That didn't sound good. What had I done?

"Have a seat, Eric," Coach Schiano said after I arrived.

I accepted his direction and waited for him to speak.

"You're probably wondering why you're here," he began, which elicited a nod from me. "I've been giving this some thought, and I'd like to move you from linebacker to defensive tackle. I think that you'll be better suited there."

After a spring of eating Nana's turkey burgers, I was down to 232 pounds—a lean-and-mean weight for any college linebacker. Now Coach was talking about putting me on the defensive line, where I'd be matched up against guys who had a good fifty-, sixty-, or even seventy-pound weight advantage on me. They'd be able to push me around pretty good.

"Really, Coach?"

"With the experience we have at linebacker, you probably wouldn't help us out this year at all," Coach Schiano said. "We want you to help us on the defensive line rotation. We believe you'll be a natural on the line."

In the trenches, he meant. The line of scrimmage was a war zone. Hand-to-hand combat. Gouging, kicking, and even punching. On the defensive line, you got down into a three-point stance every play, and when the ball was snapped, you were banging heads with giant offensive linemen, every single play.

Playing on the line was not at all glamorous compared to being a linebacker, who roams around freely and has the responsibility of tackling runners who burst through the line or dropping back into coverage. Linebackers learn to "read" the quarterback on where he's going to throw and have the opportunity to make interceptions, which often changes the complexion of the game.

"There's another thing we'd like you to do for us," Coach Schiano continued. "We think you'd make a great special teams player."

I had played on special teams before—the units that are on the field during kicking plays. At Colonia High, I was part of the kick-off return team and liked blocking for our return guy.

"We pride ourselves on our special teams at Rutgers," Coach Schiano said. "The fans might not know it, but special teams decide ball games. You can put your opponent in a bad field position, and you can take your team out of a bad field position. Knowing your role and sacrificing your ego is a key component of successful special teams play, and we think you buy into that philosophy here at Rutgers."

What could I say except, "Sure, Coach. I'll do whatever you ask of me." Although the news that my days as a linebacker were over didn't thrill me, I had always been a team player.

I had second thoughts, though, after I told one of my teammates about Coach's plans. "No, you gotta go back to Coach, E," he said. "You tell him that you want to be a linebacker and don't belong down in the trenches."

Well, I didn't think I could tell Coach Schiano that he had made a mistake and should play me at linebacker, because that would be bordering on insubordination. But I did get the nerve to ask him if I could try out being a defensive tackle for a few days, and if I didn't like it, then we could talk about returning me to the linebacker position.

"Sure, we'll see how it goes," Coach Schiano said.

Once I started playing on the line, the coaching staff kept me there. In fact, I never played a down at the linebacker position during my college career at Rutgers.

Moving Around the Line

Summer was all about team bonding. After training camp opened, we headed to a Navy SEALs leadership conference where Coach Schiano had everyone wear black bracelets with the letters F.A.M.I.L.Y.: "Forget About Me, I Love You"—another motto to go with "keep chopping." Coach wore the rubber bracelet, too.

When the regular school year started in September, I moved into the Silvers apartments, also on Busch Campus, which featured garden-style two-bedroom units with a living room, full kitchen, bath, and storage room. I roomed with Brandon Jones, a freshman defensive back and cornerback. Marquis Hamm, a defensive end, and Timothy Wright, a wide receiver, shared the other bedroom.

I can't remember a time anyone used the stove to cook something. All our meals were provided at Busch Dining Hall, so there wasn't much reason to even have a saucepan. Besides, Mom filled our kitchen cabinets and refrigerator with an assortment of snack foods: Hot Pockets, pizza rolls, bags of Tostitos chips, granola bars, and lots and lots of Gatorade. Every other week she'd make a Shop-Rite run and stock our kitchen pantry. Sometimes she'd make a pan of ziti or lasagna so that we'd have something more substantial to curb late-night hunger pangs.

I didn't have to worry about my weight any longer because now my goal was to *add* bulk. Good-bye turkey burger, hello Hot Pockets. Even though the decision that Coach wanted to play me on the defensive line was a blow, the good news was that he didn't want to redshirt me and sit me out a year before I could take the field. I couldn't imagine going an entire season without playing football.

Playing against 300-pound offensive tackles and guards was an eye-opener during practice sessions. When they grabbed me at 232 pounds, it was like they owned me. Some of them threw me around like a Raggedy Ann doll. I had to be quick and fast, more nimble, which fit into Coach Schiano's defensive philosophy—small, swift, speedy, and strong.

I decided to keep the number 52, even though I was moving to the defensive line, where players usually wore numbers in the 70s or 90s. No one on the Rutgers staff said anything about No. 52 lining up against guards and tackles during practice snaps, so I went with it.

Running out of the tunnel for my first college game was a big thrill. The cheers of more than forty thousand fans was something I had never heard in high school, but I didn't get to burn off any nervous energy playing against Fresno State in our season opener, where I warmed the bench during a game we lost.

I did see some action at defensive end against North Carolina, but we lost that game too. A 0–2 record was never how you wanted to start out a season, and a good Navy team was up next. The week before the game, we were hit with another setback: during practice, Gary Watts, a fifth-year senior defensive end, got his foot caught up in a pile-on and tore the ACL ligament in his knee. He was done for the year.

The coaches decided to move me out to defensive end to back up Jamaal Westerman (now playing for the Miami Dolphins). The

transition wasn't easy. I got pancaked twice in practice by Anthony
Davis (now an offensive tackle for the San Francisco 49ers). I'm telling you, I was surrounded by some great talent—players who were
headed to the NFL—which explains why I felt a bit overwhelmed
at times learning a new position and a new way of thinking about
playing defense.

We lost five out of our first six games. Panic set in, and Coach
Schiano decided to try something new. He didn't like the way our
fullbacks were playing, so he announced that he was moving me
over to fullback for a tryout.

Fullback, like defensive lineman, is a head-banging position
where your role is to be the lead blocker for your tailback or halfback. I was fine with grunt work, though. Anything to help the
team.

After a couple of weeks, I discovered how concussions practically went hand in hand with playing fullback at the Division I level.
In practice, you're running into people and banging heads all the
time. I was concerned: How much punishment could my body take
every single day in practice? I soldiered on, and the coaches like the
way I was blocking enough to give me playing time in games against
UConn and Pittsburgh.

But I was never handed the ball. You had to earn the ball in our
program, and the coaching staff was certainly in no mood to hand
the ball to a freshman. So I blocked as ferociously as I could and did
a good job. After a handful of games, though, I was moved back to
defensive end, which was fine with me. I was glad to no longer be a
battering ram.

With all the movement between positions, what I was really
sinking my teeth into was special teams. There are five special teams
on every squad: kickoff, kickoff return, punt, punt return, and field
goal unit. I was tapped for kickoff and kickoff return.

I especially liked playing on the kickoff team. I loved sprinting down the field, reading my keys—looking for how their kickoff team had set up for the return—and then finding the ball. I loved taking some guy out, whether it was a blocker or the return man.

When I was part of the kickoff return team, I tried to open up running lanes and blindside players whose eyes were set on nailing our return guy.

The first time I played special teams was in the third game of the season against Navy. We were returning a kickoff when I hit one of their players, and he fell on the ground. As I jogged off the field, Coach Schiano yelled at me, "Stay on your man!"

Even though I took the player out, I didn't make sure he wasn't going to get back on the field. So during the next kickoff return, I spotted the same guy. This time I hit him so hard that I later found out he got a concussion. I kept him on the ground, pushing him on his chest so that he couldn't get back up and help his team.

When I got back to the sideline, Coach Schiano congratulated me. "Good job staying on your man, but if your man is down, go find someone else to block."

A big hit can really fire up your team—and your fans. Mom remembers the time when we played Pitt midway through my freshman season at Heinz Field—home of the Pittsburgh Steelers. Mom couldn't afford to go to every out-of-town game, so she was watching my game with friends and family at a sports bar near the Rutgers campus. During a Rutgers kickoff, she watched me fly down the field and flatten the ballcarrier right after he caught the ball. Bam!

"That's my son!" she exclaimed as she slapped hands with friends.

For home games, she trained her eyes just on me—like she had done from my days of playing Pop Warner. I knew that she followed my every move on the field and on the sideline. But she had to stay focused because Coach Schiano was always shuffling players around, depending on the game situation—first, second, or third down and yards to go. Even though I wasn't playing that much on defense—around ten to fifteen plays a game—I was still on the field for all the kickoffs and kickoff returns.

What an adrenaline rush when our kicker, Teddy Dellaganna, sent the ball into the air, especially at the beginning of the game. I viewed the opening kickoff as a way to put our stamp on the game. If I made a huge hit, then I got our crowd into the game immediately. If I got the crowd into the game, then they'd holler like crazy during the first set of downs. If we made a three-and-out stop, then the opposing team would have to punt from deep in their territory. The momentum would be all on our side, especially if our offense mounted a scoring drive.

I wanted to be the tone setter. I wanted to be that guy. I wanted to get every Rutgers fan into the game—home or away.

While I was still feeling my way as a defensive lineman, I was making a name for myself on special teams. A lot of people didn't like to run full speed down the field and hit somebody.

But I did.

The vicious collisions that occur during kickoffs, however, is why these opening acts are known as the most dangerous play in football.

Tight Schedule

Playing football at a major college like Rutgers made for a very structured existence. The day started with waking up and having breakfast, usually around 8:15 or 8:30 in the morning. Then it was off to my first class at 10:05.

I initially declared communications as my major, but I was having a rough go with the entry-level Introduction to Media Systems class. I found it hard to understand the professor and the flow of the class. Fortunately, I had plenty of help as a member of the football team. I had an academic advisor that I had to meet with every day to go over my time management book and account for each hour of my day. If I didn't get my book checked, I was in big trouble.

After morning classes, I didn't have much time for a lunch break because football practice ran from 1 P.M. to 5:00 or 5:30. I had a 6:10 class that first semester, which was tough to make. I usually wolfed down something to eat before rushing to class. Somewhere during the day I had to fit in my study hall hours.

With so much going on, and having to justify every hour between waking up and 9 P.M., there wasn't any time for partying, hanging out with friends, kicking back and relaxing—whatever you want to call it.

The only time we let loose a little bit was after a win—but six weeks into the season, we were 1–5 and going nowhere fast. The mood in the locker room was miserable. My teammates were walking around in a daze, wondering what was happening to our season. Practice wasn't fun.

The cloud finally lifted when we edged UConn, 12–10. We kept the momentum going the following week against seventeenth-ranked Pittsburgh, surprising everyone with a 54–34 whooping on the road. We had our swagger back. Practice was fun again, and we kept our spirits high, winning our last six games of the regular season. It felt great to be part of such a big turnaround and long winning streak.

When people get to know me today, they say to me all the time, *Eric, you have such a big smile and are so nice to everybody. How did you play that mean game of football?*

"You should have seen me when I put my helmet on," I'll reply.

"I was a totally different person. I talked junk and everything. I was the biggest trash talker out there."

Like the time we played South Florida. We had won the coin flip against the Bulls and elected to receive the opening kickoff. I lined up for my position, which happened to be right next to the South Florida bench.

Several USF players, helmets off, started woofin'. They were yapping things like:

"Hey, fifty-two, you suck!"

"You think you're somethin'. You ain't nuthin'! You're garbage!"

"Get ready to get run over, fifty-two!"

I thought about saying something back, but then the referee blew the whistle, and the South Florida kicker lofted the ball toward the goal line.

The runback was designed to come my way, so the lead block was on my shoulders. I was looking to blindside somebody and take him out when, sure enough, the opportunity presented itself. One of the USF players wasn't looking where he should have been, and I knocked him on his butt. He tried to bounce off the ground, but I pushed him to the ground again.

My stunning hit helped widen a running lane for our returner, Devin McCourty, who sprang free and churned up the sidelines. He returned the ball sixty yards before being knocked out of bounds. Now we had great field position.

Time to rub it in a little.

I ran up USF's sideline, dancing on my tippy-toes.

"Woo-woo! Who's garbage now? Say something! You saw what I just did to your boy! Say something to me now!"

Okay, I went crazy, but that's the emotional side of football. I'm glad that Coach Schiano didn't see me pulling that stunt because he would have flipped out. But sometimes you gotta talk junk back, especially after you've heard an earful yourself. It's amazing how stuff flies out of your mouth that you would never, ever say in a regular conversation. There's something primal about going up against somebody with your full body against his full body. When you dominate him like that, it's easy to get carried away.

These are some of the emotions being played out on the field. Fans never get to see testosterone-juiced run-ins like this unless they're watching some miked-up players on an ESPN or NFL Films special. Football is a passionate game, and you can't be an unemotional bystander very long, or you'll get flattened.

Finishing Strong

When the 2008 season was over, our 7–5 record made us bowl eligible. We were assigned to the Papa John's Pizza Bowl in Birmingham, Alabama. Our opponent would be the North Carolina State Wolfpack, a team that we had never played in our long football history at Rutgers.

This would be a December 29 game, so I got to spend Christmas morning at home, where I opened my gifts—clothes and shoes— with Mom and Nicole. Then I had to check into the Hale Center at 1 P.M. for the team flight to Birmingham.

Mom and Nicole flew a couple of days later to Atlanta and then drove over to Alabama to watch the game. Mom had missed only two road games that season—the thrilling victory over Pittsburgh and a tough loss to Cincinnati—but there was no way you could keep her from attending a bowl game televised nationally on ESPN.

We came back from a 17–6 halftime deficit to mount a furious rally, and I had my hand in three stops that helped us come back in the fourth quarter to finish the 2008 season strong with a 29–23 victory over NC State.

The win made us 8–5—not too shabby for a team that was

looking down the barrel of a 1–5 start. Our seven consecutive wins raised some eyebrows around the country.

I had gained ten pounds or so during the season, so now I was playing at 242 pounds. But that still wasn't enough weight be an impact player for something other than special teams.

Coach wanted me back in the weight room after a three-week break in early January. I was fine with that.

I had never shied away from hard work before, and I wasn't about to start now.

7

THE SCARLET WALK

One of the great traditions at a tradition-rich school like Rutgers is the Scarlet Walk.

Two hours before every home game, our team would arrive at Rutgers Stadium in two buses after making a short drive from the Hyatt Regency in New Brunswick, where we spent the night in preparation.

After filing off the bus, we would stride past a statue called the "First Scarlet Knight"—a life-sized bronze statue of a nineteenth-century running back dressed in a woolen cap and carrying an overstuffed football. The monument commemorates the first college football game ever played, back in 1869.

The entire Rutgers football team, dressed in our snazzy scarlet red training outfits, would touch the First Scarlet Knight statue as we filed by. Then we'd follow a reddish-orange brick pathway to the locker room, where, along the way, cheerleaders shook their pom-poms and Rutgers fans of every age reached out to touch our hands.

The Rutgers University Marching Band—founded in 1915—contributed to the festive atmosphere of school spirit by playing one of our fight songs, "The Bells Must Ring" or "Colonel Rutgers." Hundreds, sometimes thousands, of red-clad Rutgers fans would politely clap, even cheer, as we passed by. The atmosphere was always electric. There's nothing like game day on a college campus.

I felt a sense of pride rise in my throat each time I made the pregame walk, and I always made sure to stop and give Mom a hug. You'd think my mother was the Official Team Mom from the way she exchanged high-fives with many of my teammates. They all knew her and enjoyed her infectious laugh and easy smile.

After I had lined up at three spots during my freshman year—defensive end, defensive tackle, and fullback—Coach Schiano settled on defensive tackle for my second season of college ball. Coming out of training camp, he had me and senior Charlie Noonan—a six-foot, two-inch, 295-pound defensive tackle from St. Joseph's Prep School in Philadelphia—rotating every four plays. The platoon system worked for me.

I usually lined up right on the center as the nose guard. As soon as the center snapped the ball, I had to control my gap, the A gap. There are four gaps along the line: A, B, C, and D, and then there's the large gap between the offensive line and the wide receivers.

I was in the trenches—taking my three-point stance just a couple of feet away from center where the offensive line made the initial push and the defensive line had to counter that forward surge while filling any gaps that appeared. I tried to use my strength as best as I could, but I also had to learn new techniques, like rolling off the opposing linemen and getting their hands off me. Since I was always going up against players who were bigger—and theoretically stronger—I needed to rely on technique and my superior speed to gain an advantage over my foes.

I had bulked up during the off-season to 260 pounds, but I was still light compared to teammates like Charlie Noonan. I noticed that my strength had increased, though, which meant I wasn't getting pushed around nearly as much as I did when I started my freshman year at 232 pounds. After a three-week break in January, I had gotten back into the weight room and gained eighteen more crucial pounds during the spring and early summer. While I was bulking up, I could eat my favorite foods with reckless abandon: cheeseburgers, fries, milk shakes, and Mom's homemade lasagna, which she would drop off at the Silvers apartments.

Coach Schiano felt that one of the reasons I wasn't suited for linebacker was that 230 pounds wasn't my natural weight. He said my frame was too big for 230. Coach believed I was better suited for playing football at 260–270 pounds, just the right size for one of his speedy yet strong defensive tackles. When the combination of lifting through the spring and summer and eating tons of comfort food beefed me up to that desired weight, I became more valuable to the team.

My First Start

Thanks to a resurgence in the Rutgers football program, Rutgers Stadium was expanded during the off-season, adding around eight thousand seats and a large scoreboard in the south end zone. As we headed into my sophomore year, Coach Schiano preached about looking at every game as a "one game season"—a concept that would keep us focused on the game at hand and not ahead to the one the following week. Unfortunately, we laid an egg against Cincinnati in our season-opener game, losing 47–15 before our largest home crowd ever, 53,737 people, and a nationwide audience looking in on ESPN.

I received my first career start in the fourth game of the 2009 season against the University of Maryland Terrapins. We had won two out of three games up to then, so this away game at Maryland would be a good barometer of how good we would be for the rest of the season. Mom and Nicole drove down from New Jersey to cheer me on, and I was keyed up when I ran out of the locker room as a starting player.

There was more on the line than an interconference matchup between a Big East team and an Atlantic Coast Conference upstart. Rutgers versus Maryland was bigger than that. This was Nike versus Under Armour, a Maryland company that was challenging Nike in the athletic apparel industry: uniforms, warm-ups, undershirts, and accessories like gloves and skullcaps. Fittingly, the University of Maryland was outfitted in Under Armour gear from head to toe while Rutgers rolled into College Park, Maryland, wearing our Nike gear.

Somebody at Nike must have seen that we were playing Maryland because suddenly, out of nowhere, everyone on the team received new cleats that week—red cleats with the Nike swoosh. The fact that the game was on national TV probably had something to do with it. It's all about exposure, and red cleats stand out—like my first pair of cherry-red Nike Air Hyperflights certainly did back in the day.

Both programs wanted to shine and win bragging rights with recruits along the eastern seaboard, so there was plenty at stake on a drab, rainy Saturday afternoon at Byrd Stadium when our new red cleats quickly got muddy on the Bermuda grass field. We didn't let a little rain or mud stop us, however.

In the middle of the second quarter in a 10–10 game, the Terps' offensive guard and the center must have gotten their signals crossed because they left the A gap wide open for me. When their quarterback, Chris Turner, dropped back to pass, I was in his kitchen before he even finished his seven-step drop. Turner saw me coming and huddled into a ball to absorb the hit he was going to receive. I bowled into him, wrapped my arms around his shoulders, and dumped him on the ground for a six-yard loss to record my first-ever sack.

Even though it was a first-down play on Maryland's own 31-yard line in the second quarter, I felt like I had made a fourth-down goal-line stop to save a victory. I jumped up and began chopping my right forearm so rapidly that I could have felled one of those trees in the forest that Coach Schiano was always talking about. I was wild with excitement and could barely keep a lid on the joy bubbling to the surface.

A couple of my teammates immediately surrounded me with arms outstretched, telling me to cool it and deflect attention from the fact that I was chopping. In this case, no flag was thrown. Maybe the refs were looking the other way.

Next thing I knew, I was being replaced by Blair Bines and jogging back to the sidelines, where Coach Schiano was waiting for me.

He tore off his headset and got in my face. "Celebrate with your team!" he yelled. "Don't be an individual out there, or you'll get a flag!"

He was right, of course. There was a line that I couldn't cross with the refs, and I had certainly bumped up right next to it, chopping and calling attention to myself. I was lucky there wasn't a yellow flag tossed high into the air for "excessive celebration," which would have cost us fifteen yards and an automatic first down in a tie game. Instead, we had the Terrapins pinned back on their 24-yard line, second down and sixteen yards to go.

Advantage Rutgers. Sure enough, Maryland quarterback Chris Turner tried to get it all back on the next play and threw into coverage, where our DB Devin McCourty intercepted the ball at midfield.

We played a great second half to take a 27–13 lead into the fourth quarter. Maryland got the ball back with just under five minutes to go, but any dreams of coming back to tie us were snuffed when I sacked Turner for an eight-yard loss at the Maryland 16-yard line. This time I *did* celebrate with my team by exchanging the usual hand slaps and fist bumps. We won going away, 34–13.

I still keep a memento from that game. A sideline photographer took a great photo of me chopping away during that first-half sack. After my spinal cord injury, we had that photo blown up to a life-size cutout and mounted on my bedroom wall. Whenever I have visitors, I love telling the story.

Fat Sandwiches

Less than two weeks after the Maryland victory, I was featured in a Q&A in the sports section of the *Daily Targum*, the Rutgers student newspaper. Correspondent Steve Miller interviewed me for his column. I guess they thought with my play on the field getting more attention, the student body would be interested in learning more about me.

STEVE MILLER: Between *NCAA Football* and *Madden*, which is your [video] game of choice?

ERIC LEGRAND: *Madden*, definitely.

SM: Which team do you play with?

EL: The Broncos—the Denver Broncos.

SM: Are you a Broncos fan? And who is your favorite player?

EL: Of course, I'm a Broncos fan. It's the Broncos all day. My favorite player used to be Terrell Davis, but now I don't know—maybe D. J. Williams is my favorite player now. I wore No. 30 in high school for Terrell Davis.

SM: What was the first thing you ever got at the grease trucks?

EL: The "Fat Biddie Boy" with no marina sauce . . . no, it was a cheeseburger with French fries.

SM: If you could name your own fat sandwich and put anything on it, what would it be?

EL: I don't think I'd make one. I like my "Fat Biddie Boy" with no marinara sauce but with ketchup.

SM: What's your favorite sports movie?

EL: I'd say *Friday Night Lights*.

SM: If you played any sports other than football, what would it be?

EL: Baseball. I played that just as much as I played football growing up, but I quit in high school when Rutgers offered me a scholarship.

SM: What position did you play?

EL: I was a center fielder and pitcher.

SM: What was your best pitch?

EL: The splitter.

Good thing Steve Miller didn't ask me if I ever nailed anyone with my wild pitches.

When the article came out, my friends teased me about my answer to the "grease trucks" question—the "grease trucks" being a group of truck-based food vendors located on College Avenue that were absolutely legendary on campus. Rutgers students flocked to these colorful food trucks—some were named RU Hungry?, Just Delicious, and Mr. C's—for every sort of fried food under the sun, but their calling cards were an assortment of "fat sandwiches" consisting of a white sub rolls stuffed with items like burger meat, chicken fingers, gyro meat, pork roll, bacon, mozzarella sticks, and french fries.

This was the epitome of college food, an awesome sandwich

for six or seven bucks that was guaranteed to clog your arteries but so worth it. (A dietician discovered that a typical fat sandwich had 1,718 calories with 78 grams of fat.) My favorite on-the-go-meal or late-night snack was the Fat Biddie Boy, which contained grilled chicken, cheeseburger, mozzarella sticks, and fries, but instead of having these worthy ingredients slathered with marinara sauce, I preferred ketchup. It's been said that you're not really a Rutgers student until you've had a fat sandwich.

My roommates and I loved the occasional late-night run for a fat sandwich. I lived with three players from Long Island my sophomore year—Scott Vallone, Devon Watkis, and Beau Bachety—and we called ourselves the 168 Crew because that was the apartment number that we lived in.

Scott, at six feet, three inches and 275 pounds, played defensive tackle; DWat was a six-foot, seven-inch, 316-pound backup offensive lineman who was a gentle giant—more gentle than me; and Beau was a six-foot, four-inch, 260-pound tight end. We were an ebony-and-ivory apartment: two black kids and two white kids, and we became very close, bonding over our late-night video game obsession.

Many times after an hour or two of playing WWE Wrestling, we would try some of the wrestling moves on each other in our dorm apartment. We'd get on the floor and try to pin each other with one of the guys pretending he was the referee and counting one, two . . . before the guy getting pinned would throw off the aggressor. Like my roomies, I had grown up watching wrestling on TV and loved it. I always thought the sport was real as a little kid and was really into the Rock and Kane.

One night, I talked Devon into trying a finishing move known as the Pedigree, which was the signature move popularized by the wrestler Triple H. With a healthy weight advantage of 316 pounds, DWat was game.

We cleared out the living room couches to make some room and put pillows on the floor. Devon knew the choreography of the Pedigree: he would charge me, and then I would kick him in the stomach, at which point he would fall forward a little bit, giving me a chance to grab his two arms and perform a move known as a double underhook where I would pin both arms behind his back. At the same time, he would put his head between my legs, I would jump, release his arms, and perform a kneeling or sitout face-buster.

Scott and Beau egged us on to try the Pedigree, so we went for it. We did all the right choreographed moves, and then when I jumped into the air with his head between my knees, we hit the ground at the same time. The next thing I knew, my face slammed into his back, which really did a number on my nose.

The shot of pain! I thought I had broken my nose, but my room-mates were howling because our Pedigree move looked so real. I fell on my back and moaned—until I suddenly "revived" and leaped on Devon and pummeled him just like they did on TV.

We were always doing crazy stuff like that. Every Thursday the guys and I would head over to Applebee's at 10 P.M., when appetizers were half off. The four of us would fill up a booth and start yapping away. Usually, we would pick up from the conversation we had a week before, which was basically Scott, DWat, and Beau—who were from New York—telling me that New Jersey sucks.

"Why did you come here then?" I would ask.

"Because it was the only major Division 1 college close to us," one of them would say.

"You could have gone to Syracuse."

"Bro, that is like five hours away."

We would go back and forth like that with me defending the Garden State, and my roomies making fun of how you can't pump your own gas in New Jersey or telling me that the only thing that grows in my home state is the crime rate. Or how state parks are always found in our toxic waste dumps.

Thankfully, the food would arrive to stop the bickering. I always started with fried mozzarella sticks; that was my appetizer. After that, my cheeseburger with a side order of fries would arrive. I ordered my burger well done with no rabbit food on the side. Lettuce, tomato, or pickles were not for me. To accompany my meal, I ordered a chocolate milk shake, and dessert was the triple chocolate meltdown.

Looking back at these times, they seem so carefree. Goofing around with the guys, enjoying the life of a typical college student. Thankfully, playing college football gave me structure I needed to keep on track, and my focus on the game was stronger than ever.

Special Teams Play

We had won four out of five games when Pittsburgh, an up-and-coming team that had won five of their first six games, rolled into Piscataway. Once again we would be playing in our newly expanded stadium, and once again we would be televised on ESPN for this special Friday night game. Coach Schiano repeated his refrain about the importance of a "one-game season."

It was all for naught. We lost, 24–17, but what sticks in my mind is how even though we took a 7–0 lead and had all the momentum we needed, our kickoff team allowed Pittsburgh's Ray Graham to make a 54-yard return, which set up a short drive to even the score. As Coach Schiano always said, if you let your opponent make a long runback, you're sucking the emotion out of your team. There's no air in your sails after they pin a long runback against your kickoff team.

Our ninth game of the season was also on ESPN—a Thursday

night matchup against 23rd-ranked South Florida. Playing at home on national TV for the third time that fall seemed to be the charm. We killed the Bulls, 31–0, and it felt great to be part of a defense that shut out a high-scoring team that had gotten on the scoreboard in every regular-season game in its thirteen-year history. Our impressive win made us bowl-eligible for the fifth season in a row.

We ended the season with losses to Big East rivals Syracuse and West Virginia. But where I shined was on kickoff coverage. I led the team with thirteen tackles on kickoffs, and more often than not, good things happened when I made a stop inside the 20-yard line.

Our losses to Syracuse and West Virginia dropped us to 8–4, still qualifying us for the St. Petersburg Bowl in Florida. Going to the bowl game was a chance to get some early Christmas presents: the swag they gave each player was awesome—a Flip video camera, backpack, T-shirts, shorts, sneakers, and other goodies.

The St. Petersburg Bowl pitted the University of Central Florida Knights against the Rutgers Scarlet Knights, two 8–4 teams. This bowl game felt like a road game, however, because 20,000 UCF fans were among the crowd of 29,763 at Tropicana Field. We gave their fans something to cheer about on the opening kickoff when Quincy McDuffie of Central Florida ran past us for 65 yards all the way down to our 31-yard line. I slapped my hands in frustration because I had a chance to make a tackle but I got blocked at the last second. Our kickoff team hung our heads a bit as we jogged toward our sideline with the sounds of the UCF school band playing their fight song.

It looked like Central Florida had the momentum, but then our linebacker Damaso Munoz made a big interception, and we were back in business. We ended up kicking off a lot that game—eight times—as we ran over Central Florida, 45–24. Two of these kickoffs stand out in my mind.

In the first, I had a bead on the Knights' Quincy McDuffie and gave him a good lick. He bounced off the field and started talking trash. "Boy, you don't hit hard!" he yelled.

I wasn't going to stand for that. "I just knocked you five yards from the place I hit you. Shut up and get off the field!"

The next time we kicked off, you can be sure I wanted his number, and this time I hit him much harder. We exchanged more trash talk, but at the end of the night the score did the talking. We won our fourth bowl game in the last four years and gave our fans who made the trip to Florida a nice plane ride home.

Nine-and-four was quite an accomplishment, but the 2009 season could have been better. For decades, Rutgers fans would have thrown a parade for us down College Avenue after going 9–4, and we would have celebrated by eating fat sandwiches. But after five years of success, Rutgers fans were hungrier for even greater success.

So was everyone on the team. We all felt there was some unfinished business. We all knew something special would happen next season, my junior year.

Getting Wheels

As the sophomore season wrapped up, I was in the process of getting my first car. I had waited for my first ride for a *long* time, but Mom never had the money.

It was up to me to buy my first car, so I carefully saved up money from birthday and graduation gifts and put away any extra left over from my stipend to attend Rutgers. (My only indulgence was the occasional Fat Biddie Boy and Thursday nights at Applebee's.) I had also saved a chunk of money from working at a Christmas tree lot during my senior year of high school. I made nice tips tying trees to the roofs of cars and sending people on their way.

With five thousand dollars resting in the bank, I hoped to have enough to get the car I wanted: a 2002 Nissan Altima. Mom and I kept our eyes out on Craigslist and ads in the *Star-Ledger*. We eventually found what I was looking for at a car dealer in Atlantic Highlands, which is along the shore just south of New York City. The 2002 Nissan Altima was in the color I wanted: black. There were 95,000 miles on the odometer. The price was five thousand dollars, exactly my budget.

Mom volunteered to drive down to the dealership and purchase the car so I wouldn't miss any classes. After taking a test drive and checking out the car, she signed the papers and drove the used Altima off the lot. The plan was that she would drive to New Brunswick, and then we'd drive back together to Atlantic Highlands to pick up her car.

On the way back to the car dealership, it started raining on Highway 35. We were about two miles from the car dealer when a young woman in the fast lane slammed on the brakes. Someone had cut her off, but her reaction was to come to a complete stop in the fast lane of a fast-moving highway.

There was nowhere for me to go. I slammed on my brakes, but this time I didn't stop in time. I slid right into her, crinkling her rear fender and doing a good number on my front bumper assembly. And then another car—a van—plowed into us, almost at full speed. Our air bags didn't deploy, but the back window exploded into shards of glass. Our crumpled sedan was pushed into the median, where it sustained more bumps and bruises. Glass was everywhere, even in our front seat. Thank goodness we weren't injured, but I sat there in total shock. The car that I had owned for a couple of hours—and invested my life savings in—was now a total wreck.

Mom was hysterical, no doubt flashing back to the car accident that claimed her brother's life.

"Mom, relax. We're going to be fine. This car wasn't meant to be."

"How can you be so calm?" she asked, brushing away tears. "We just bought this car, and now it's totaled!"

"Relax, Mom. There's nothing we can do now."

I displayed a calmness, an unruffled manner that portended a more serious accident only six months away. My new car was totaled the same afternoon I purchased it, and there was nothing we could do to go back in time.

We had the car towed back to the dealership, and let's just say you should have seen the look on the salesman's face.

Long story short, Mom had taken out only liability insurance on the car but no collision insurance, so we had to go after the owner of the van that struck us from behind. Eventually, after a lot of fighting, we got back our five thousand dollars.

As soon as we received the insurance money, Mom and I started looking for a new used car. We soon found another 2002 Nissan Altima, but this one had fewer miles: just 67,000. The dealer wanted around $8,500 for it, but we explained the situation and said that five thousand was all I had. The car salesman "sharpened his pencil" and lowered the price to six thousand *and* offered to throw in new tires and a tune-up. I was still a thousand dollars short, but Mom graciously agreed to cover the difference.

That was my mother, always digging deep for me.

"See, Mom? There was something about that other car," I said before I left for Rutgers. "I guess we weren't supposed to have that one. Look—now we found this new car, and we got a better deal. For a thousand dollars more, we got a car with thirty thousand fewer miles. They also gave us four new tires and a tune-up."

That's what I was always doing—looking at the bright side. Little did I know that in less than half a year, I would never drive that car again.

Meeting a Special Young Woman

———

After the 2009 football season was over, I noticed that a lot of the football guys were mingling with the soccer girls. There was D. C. Jefferson, who was dating a forward on the Rutgers women's soccer team. My roommate Scott Vallone was trying to get the cell phone number of one of the soccer players as well.

I was always cool with Rheanne Sleiman, from North Vancouver, British Columbia, who was a member of Canada's national U20 team for players under twenty years of age. She was one of four Canadians recruited to play at Rutgers.

I first noticed Rheanne during the middle of my freshman year. I saw her at the Hale Center, where we had our weight room and study hall. She caught my eye, and I said hello to her. Later I messaged her on Facebook: "One day, you're going to let me use your car." It was all a joke, but I was still without wheels at that point.

I liked her answer back: "I don't know if you can handle my car." Rheanne drove a sporty Mazda 3.

We quickly became friends, and she would come over to hang out with my roommates, and then we'd all go to the movies or out to eat.

When my freshman year was over, Rheanne went back home to Canada while I remained on campus for the summer session. I lived in a house near campus and shared an upstairs bedroom with Devon Watkins. Our other roommate was Shamar Graves, the Woodbridge High player who the Rutgers coaching staff was looking at when Coach Susan "discovered" me after my freshman year of high school.

The house had no air-conditioning, so Devon and I would bake up there every single night in the summer heat. Devon had purchased a big fan, which he would point in his direction as he went to bed. When he fell asleep, I'd reach over and point the fan toward me. Sometime during the hot and humid night, he'd wake up sweating and point his fan back toward himself. At the first inkling of dawn, I'd point the fan toward myself. These antics helped us get through the hot summer.

When Rheanne returned from Canada and began practice with the women's soccer team, we continued to see each other a lot but always as "friends" just hanging out. I liked her because she was funny, outgoing, and easy to get along with and talk to about anything. Rheanne had a sunny personality, and she always looked at the bright side, just like me.

It was on one particular occasion after my sophomore season when I started to develop feelings for her. Rheanne was upset because she received a bad grade in one of her classes. She was homesick and needed someone to talk to, so I was that friend for her. Being there for her on that night brought us closer. I still continued to tell my buddies that we were *just friends,* but I eventually summoned the courage to take things to the next level.

I knew this was an important step in our relationship because if she preferred to remain "just friends," things could get awkward.

"Rheanne, will you go out with me?" I asked one night when she was hanging out at our apartment. I'll never forget the day: May 5, 2010.

She got all excited and said without hesitation, "Yeah." Then she started giggling like a schoolgirl.

When our friends heard what happened, the reaction was, *Gee, finally. It's about time.* We didn't have to spend any time getting to know each other because we had already done that. It was like we had been friends forever.

I had dated before, but not much. My first girlfriend was when I was in seventh grade, and I had a couple more in middle school. I had a girlfriend at the end of my junior year into my senior of high school, and then I had a long-distance relationship with a girl from Chicago that ended soon after I started college at Rutgers. I didn't have any girlfriends at Rutgers until I started hanging with Rheanne. I think I was just focused on football more than anything else.

When it came to dating, racial and ethnic background didn't matter to me. A couple of my girlfriends in middle school were half black or half Latino. My third girlfriend was Italian, my fourth was of Greek heritage, and my fifth was of German ancestry. Rheanne had a Lebanese father and a French Canadian–Irish mother. Skin color wasn't important to me; I just wanted my girlfriends to be pretty, and Rheanne with her long, curly black hair was certainly that. If you like me and I like you and we have stuff in common, hey, who knows where it can go?

Mom was always supportive no matter whom I dated, and Rheanne's parents were cool when they heard that Rheanne and I had become an item. It was good to hear I didn't have anything to worry about in that department.

When the spring semester was over, Rheanne flew home to Vancouver, as she always did at the end of the school year. I was upset to see her go because by then we were seeing each other every day. Thank goodness for cell phones and Skype so that we could continue to stay in close contact.

She returned to New Brunswick just before I started training camp in August. It felt amazing to see her regularly again and have her close. I had stayed on campus because I had summer school and weight-training sessions to get ready for my junior year.

Everyone was telling me that I was a rising star in the Rutgers program, and my junior season would be my breakout year. I was ready. It had always been my dream as a little kid to go to the NFL and then retire and become a sports broadcaster, so if I was going to play football in the pros, I needed a big year.

I finally felt settled in at nose guard. I had played that one position all my sophomore year, and I knew what I had to do to become an impact player.

Coach Schiano still wanted me on special teams. In fact, he saw me as the catalyst of the kickoff team, the chairman of the boards who set the tone. Now that I was going to be a junior, I could take even more of a leadership role.

I was also aware that NFL scouts look at *everything*—every play, including the kickoffs. Maybe they'd see some guy flying down the field, knocking blockers down right and left in a relentless pursuit of the kickoff returner. Maybe they'd see a player who was fearless against a wedge of blockers, a player who always got his man.

Maybe they'd be like those Rutgers coaches who—during my freshman year of high school football—looked at game tape of another player and saw someone else making plays right and left. Maybe the NFL scouts would look at tape of my Rutgers games and say, "Who is that guy?"

I wanted them to find out.

8

THE LEAD-UP TO GAME TIME

The 2010 football season would be Coach Greg Schiano's tenth at the helm of the Rutgers team, and while many Scarlet Knight fans appreciated how Coach had turned around a losing program that was once a national laughingstock, a vocal minority wanted to see a Big East conference championship year in and year out.

We didn't know what to expect for the 2010 season. Some preseason pundits were saying that we could be in a "rebuilding year" despite 8–5 and 9–4 seasons in 2008 and 2009, while others believed we could be a Top 25 team and contend for the Big East championship.

Which way would the ball bounce?

I knew our defense would have to carry this team, but I thought our D was up to the task. We ranked right up there with the top programs during my sophomore year: we were No. 2 nationally in turnover margin, No. 4 in sacks, No. 15 against the run, No. 16 in scoring, and No. 18 in overall defense (out of 120 teams). Coach Schiano had us in an aggressive mind-set, and he liked to pull the trigger with blitzes. There was a great spirit on our side of the ball.

Although I had played nose guard throughout my sophomore year, Coach Schiano tweaked my position for the new season. He put me into a three-man rotation with Charlie Noonan, who played nose guard, and my roommate Scott Vallone, who played defensive tackle. The three of us would rotate between nose guard and defensive tackle.

Under this new system, Charlie and Scott would start off and play four or five plays, and then I would go in as a nose guard with Charlie coming off the field. Then I would rotate over to Scott's position at defensive tackle and Charlie would come back in at nose guard. We were three men sharing two positions. It was innovative, kept us physically fresh, and forced opposing offenses to make adjustments for us.

Coach Schiano also decided to shake things up with the way we practiced. Every football team I had ever played on always practiced in the afternoon. Rutgers was no different. After morning classes, the players were expected to arrive at Hale Center at one o'clock, where a box lunch would be waiting for us in our lockers. We'd eat, get dressed, and go upstairs for a team meeting. Coach Schiano would talk about the practice the day before and what we needed to accomplish that day. Then we'd break up into a position meeting, where I gathered with other defensive linemen and defensive team coaches to watch film of our practice from the day before.

Talk about accountability. You could never loaf in practice.

Around 2:45, we'd start—warm-up, practice drills, offense versus defense scrimmage, and conditioning work. Depending on the weather, we either practiced outside or inside under a bubble dome. We'd usually wrap up by 5:15—or 5:30 at the latest—since a majority of players had night classes. After a dinner break, those who didn't have night classes were expected to attend study hall and watch film of our next opponent.

There was no chance for downtime with that schedule. It was go-go-go until nine o'clock, when you could take a deep breath and wind down from the long day. It was a grind for the players.

Coach Schiano believed we were rushed throughout the day, and he was right. It did seem like we always had somewhere to go or somewhere to be. His solution: practice early in the morning.

Real early. As in starting-at-6-A.M. early. At first, my teammates couldn't believe that Coach was doing this. College students weren't used to getting up at the crack of dawn. We were all night owls, and we all had friends who pulled all-nighters.

But six o'clock was when we had to check in at the Hale Center for breakfast. After we were finished eating, we'd head downstairs to the locker room, where we would dress for our 7:15 team meeting. And then practice would follow the same schedule that we had for afternoons. We'd be off the field by 11:30 or 11:45.

Coach was always thinking proactively and outside the box. He also stressed the importance of giving back to the community, asking each team member to volunteer his time for a worthy cause.

Beau Bachety and Devon Watkis chose to volunteer their time visiting children at Robert Wood Johnson University Hospital and Saint Peter's University Hospital in New Brunswick. They wore their scarlet Rutgers jerseys and called on brave children fighting life-threatening diseases like leukemia. Our players liked hanging out with the children, autographing Rutgers T-shirts, and posing for pictures. I hear they did an awesome job.

I chose the Special Olympics as my cause. During the summer leading into my junior season, I was among the twenty-six Scarlet Knights who helped kick off the 2010 Special Olympics with the opening ceremonies at the College of New Jersey (TCNJ). Each player walked with special athletes from the New Jersey county he came from: I was representing Middlesex County, so I accompanied a handful of participants from near my hometown. (If you were a Rutgers player from outside New Jersey, the organization assigned you to a county.)

Coach Schiano served as the honorary coach for Special Olympics and delivered an inspirational speech to open the games. Being part of the Special Olympics meant a lot to me because I felt we were changing lives. The participants looked up to me as an athlete in my red No. 52 jersey. Despite their physical limitations, they were willing to get out there and do their best. I loved their smiles, and from that summer on, I decided that I would always be a Special Olympics advocate.

Just one year later, Coach Schiano was unable to make the opening ceremonies because of a family conflict. I filled in for Coach and led the opening ceremony parade into the stadium, after which I addressed the athletes and their families from a stage lined with yellow mums.

This time, though, I spoke from my wheelchair.

Early Birds

There was a lot of grumbling among the players about moving practice to early mornings. When that alarm clock went off every day, I wanted to shoot the thing. But once I got going, got some breakfast in my stomach, and suited up for practice, I had a lot of energy to take on the day. And when the horn blew to mark the end of practice, that was the best feeling, too.

I didn't have classes until 5 P.M., which gave me a good four to five hours to do whatever I wanted to do: go to study hall, watch game film of the other team, hang out with Rheanne, or go home and play *FIFA*—the video soccer game and my new favorite—on my

Xbox 360. Or I could take a nap. There were days when I needed a refreshing snooze.

As a junior, I lived off-campus with Devon Watkis and Khaseem Greene, a linebacker from Elizabeth, New Jersey. We leased a house where I had my own bedroom and a nice queen-sized bed. Oh, and I should mention my first flat-screen TV, which Mom and Nicole got for me as an early birthday present. Getting our own place was a good way to teach me to manage my money because I had to help with the bills.

Even though there were changes in my life—practice times, my responsibilities on defense—one thing was constant for me with Rutgers football: my role on special teams. I heard Coach Schiano tell his assistants that my abilities on kickoff and kickoff return were assets that he didn't want to take away from the team. I was our main man, the guy running down the field cracking heads and making a statement. I had always loved special teams and the camaraderie among us. There's no other place I wanted to be when we were kicking off or receiving. Special teams were my forte.

The big question mark heading into my junior season was our offense. We struggled to move the ball in 2009, ranking far lower nationally than our stout defense. We were 89th in passing offense and 97th in total offense. It would be up to the defense to keep things close or hold on to a slim lead. In close games, special teams were often the difference between winning and losing, which is another reason why I took my responsibilities on the kickoff and kickoff return teams so seriously.

We started off the season with a soft touch on the schedule, a game against Norfolk State, a Division 1-AA school where the players are smaller and, presumably, not as talented. We played at home on a Thursday night before a big crowd, but we didn't give our fans much to cheer about. Our offense couldn't get untracked, and we were only leading 6–0 at the half.

We eventually put Norfolk State away, 31–0, but it wasn't pretty. I played well on special teams and didn't allow the Spartans any big runbacks on a half-dozen kickoff returns, but I didn't play much on defense. I thought we were going to implement the new rotation, but my defensive coaches barely called my name.

The same thing happened against a lightly regarded Division 1 school, Florida International. We squeaked out a 19–14 win, but our offense continued to misfire. Although we won and had a 2–0 record, I was kind of down afterward since I didn't get to contribute much on defense. Some rotation plan.

Two days later, Coach Schiano called me up to his office. At first, I wondered what I had done wrong, but Coach quickly put me at ease. "I was breaking down the film, and I realized that you've barely played this year. We're going to fix that," Coach said. He explained that our new defensive line coach didn't understand the rotation system that he had installed into the game plan for Charlie, Scott, and myself.

"Don't worry," Coach said. "You're going to be seeing a lot of action from here on out. We need you out there."

It was great to hear Coach express confidence in me because I had started to question why I wasn't playing. Now I could turn my full attention to our next opponent, North Carolina. The feeling on the Rutgers team was that this game against the Tar Heels would reveal how good we really were.

Our offense, led by quarterback Tom Savage, sputtered against North Carolina. We couldn't run the ball, and our passing game couldn't get untracked. Even though we led 10–7 at the half against North Carolina, we should have been ahead by two touchdowns. Time and again, the defense came up with big stops, producing turnovers to keep things close. I played a lot of snaps this time around.

We fell behind 17–13, but we were knocking on the door at the 6-yard line midway through the fourth quarter. Then disaster struck when Tom was intercepted on a poorly thrown pass on the 7-yard line. I rushed onto the field with the defense, and we held them to a three-and-out. A short punt had us back in business on the Tar Heels' 34-yard line—great field position—but three incompletes and a sack meant we had to swallow a tough loss.

There was a lot of frustration in the locker room afterward because we had been pointing toward the North Carolina game since training camp started. It was like someone ripped the hearts out of our chests. We wanted to get back at them for whooping us on our home field my freshman year. But the plain truth is that we made too many mistakes, and they capitalized on them.

Then it was Groundhog Day all over again the following week: we lost our Homecoming Game to Tulane by a nearly identical score, 17–14. Once again we couldn't run and couldn't complete enough passes. Tom Savage was injured and replaced by true freshman quarterback Chas Dodd—meaning he didn't redshirt during his first year of college. Tom performed well but threw a pick on our last drive of the game. The aggravation worsened when our kickoff return team sprung Joe Lefeged for a 95-yard return for a touchdown, but the scoring play was nullified by a holding penalty.

Coach had asked me the day before if I would join him, a couple of coaches, and two high school recruits from Pittsburgh after the game. This would be a great opportunity for me to do my part to build up the program at Rutgers. Following a steak dinner, Coach asked me to show the recruits around town.

I explained to the recruits that after we lose a tough game like that, nobody is in a mood to party. But we did drop by a party at a friend's house, even though the mood was anything but celebratory.

"Do you guys want to go back to the hotel?" I asked after a short time.

"Sure," said one recruit.

On the way back, I explained things this way: "When we win,

it's a good time around here, but when we lose, we really take it personally and get upset."

"Yeah, we understand," said the other recruit.

I dropped them off at the hotel and then went back home to sleep.

I'll admit the Scarlet Knights were reeling after that pair of defeats. We could have been undefeated, but *coulda* and *shoulda* don't count for much in football. We had to regroup quickly because we were playing the University of Connecticut on a Friday night on ESPN—and a national TV audience would be looking in.

Our great fans were always more crazy at televised night games, too. For the UConn game, they organized a "blackout," which meant they would all arrive at Rutgers Stadium dressed in black T-shirts. There was something very intimidating about the wall of black the fans created in the stands. I knew our student section— some holding cardboard axes they used to "chop" after a big play— would be really fired up. I'll take our "twelfth man" over any other student body.

We got things going our way in the first quarter with a quick stop on defense, which put the football into the hands of Chas Dodd, who was still subbing for the injured Tom Savage. Chas wasn't afraid to take shots down the field; he was an aggressive playmaker who could make things happen. He was a competitor.

On the first set of downs, Chas dropped back and flung a 46-yard touchdown pass to give us a 7–0 lead—a great start for an offense that didn't have many long bombs or long runs up to this point. Now we were kicking off. San San Te's kick sailed toward the left—my side of the field.

I sprinted toward the end zone, but I had a double team coming at me. My job was to either split the double team, which means go through it, or stay to the outside. Instead I tried a fancy move and moved inside, but two blockers pushed me all the way inside, which opened up a huge hole. Next thing I knew, I heard their fans going crazy as UConn's Nick Williams cut back through the hole and ran untouched on a 100-yard touchdown sprint. Just like that, it was 7–7, and our early lead was history.

I was fuming. A year earlier, UConn had another 100-yard run for a touchdown against us, and now this.

"Receiving team!" bellowed our special team coach, Robb Smith.

I was back on the field with the kickoff receiving team. I think everyone felt a bit ticked by UConn's coast-to-coast touchdown run. This time it was our turn to create a running lane for Joe Lefeged. I had a key block that sprung him loose, and Joe nearly went all the way. He was chased down on UConn's 14-yard line after dashing for 75 yards, and I remember running after him, screaming in delight after taking it back on UConn.

Rutgers versus UConn turned out to be one of those lead-changing contests between two well-matched teams. We found ourselves down a touchdown with under four minutes to go. Crunch time. Our young quarterback Chas Dodd stepped up and threw a 52-yard touchdown pass to tie the game 24–24, and then Chas connected on a 45-yard pass to set up the game-winning field goal. San San Te popped the ball through the uprights from 34 yards to give us our first lead with just 13 seconds left to play, and moments later we ran off the field with helmets high celebrating a 27–24 victory.

An epic home win like that made me feel a lot better, but I knew we couldn't let mistakes on special teams happen again—not if we were going to make this a special season.

Army Rations

Coach Schiano was tough on me during the week of practice leading up to our next game against Army. But it wasn't because of the long touchdown run by UConn following our kickoff.

Every year, Coach changed the defense whenever we played one of the service academies, Army or Navy. This time around, Coach wanted me to take a certain pivot step with my left or my right foot, depending on what side of the center I was on. It's rather complicated to describe, but Coach instructed me to "read and react" to the direction the guard in front of me was going.

If their offensive guard went "out"—meaning he left his place on the line to block someone else—I had to resist the urge to follow him with my eyes but instead keep my vision focused on the gap he had just vacated. If the guard went "in," meaning he stayed put and tried to block me, I had to ride him and win the position battle. If he veered up a little bit to take me in a different direction, then I would have to push him off and watch for the center coming back at me.

All these variations would happen in a half second, literally a blink of an eye. From this initial half-second read, I had to know exactly where to go. I wasn't finding this part of the game easy. It was natural for my eyes to follow the guard because he was my man. But sometimes the guard was a decoy, and his job was to block me or keep me confused on where the play was going.

I studied these moves on film and thought I had them down, but in practice I had problems with my reads and pivoting my feet. Each time I made a mistake, Coach Schiano was all over me. He wasn't upset, but he wasn't letting anything slide.

Thankfully I was in much better shape by Thursday's practice. I had watched enough film by then to know what to look for, so my pivot steps were much better. I knew I'd be ready to play on Saturday afternoon.

Our game against Army was a continuation of a series that began in 1891, and this would be the thirty-seventh time the two teams had met. Talk about evenly matched: our series was tied, 18–18. Even though this would be a home game for us, we wouldn't be playing at Rutgers Stadium. Instead the game was set for the New Meadowlands Stadium in East Rutherford, New Jersey. The rationale behind playing at New Meadowlands—about an hour's drive from Piscataway—was purely financial. The New Meadowlands Stadium Corporation offered Rutgers $2.7 million to bring the game to the new stadium, money that would help fund other sports programs at Rutgers—like Rheanne's soccer team.

The reason that the word *New* was in front of *Meadowlands* was that the stadium had just opened a few months earlier. Built at a cost of $1.6 billion, the New Meadowlands Stadium was the home of the New York Jets and New York Giants and replaced the aging Giants Stadium, located on the same site. The new stadium seated 82,566 and came with all the bells and whistles. There were twenty giant high-def LED pylons at the north and east entrances that displayed videos of the players from both teams.

The Rutgers team stayed at the Hyatt Regency in New Brunswick, as per our custom every night before a home game. I usually roomed with Scott Vallone, but Coach Schiano wanted me to stay with Michael Larrow, a six-foot, three-inch, 258-pound defensive end who was a true freshman. The coaching staff asked me to mentor Michael, help him get mentally prepared for the game. He was still feeling his way with big-time Division I football.

Actually, I was a bit upset that my routine was thrown off. Not that I didn't want to help Michael, but Scott and I had been football game roommates for a couple of seasons, and that was the pregame routine I was used to.

Breakfast wasn't served until 8:30, so we were allowed to sleep in until 8 A.M., which, after nearly two months of early morning practice, felt like a luxury. I liked to keep breakfast light because there was always a pregame meal, so I had a toasted bagel with butter and a bowl of my favorite cereal, Kellogg's Frosted Flakes. That would last me until our pregame meal at 10:15 A.M. Game time was set for 2 P.M.

There were the usual pregame nerves that morning—a mixture of excitement coupled with a focused attitude. We were going to war with a team that wanted to do the same thing we were trying to do—win a game.

After breakfast, we assembled in hotel conference rooms for our offense and defense meetings. Nothing unusual was discussed. Our defensive team coaches reviewed the adjustments we had made during the week for Army. They were having a good season: the Black Knights were riding high with a 4–2 record, while we were 3–2. It was the first time since 1993 that both teams entered the game with winning records.

Going into the game, Army was coming off a big 41–23 road win against Tulane—a team we had lost to two weeks previously—so the Battle of the Knights was a toss-up. With just one turnover in the last four games, Army was playing solid football. Their sophomore quarterback, Trent Steelman, who had started every game since he arrived at West Point, was a good asset for their team. Meanwhile, Chas Dodd was coming off his debut game against UConn and was playing with a great deal of confidence.

After our defensive team meeting, we had a fifteen-minute break before our pregame meal, so I went back to my room and opened my playbook to review our defensive formations and blitzes. I put on my headphones and listened to Lil Wayne on my iPod—I liked how hip-hop music pumped me up before big games, and Lil Wayne was one of my favorites.

A few minutes before 10:15 A.M., I went downstairs for our pregame meal. We were a little less than four hours before the opening kickoff—a time when you zone in. No more joking around or laughing. Cell phones turned off. Time to get locked and loaded.

I ate what I always did right before a game: lasagna, a piece of bread, and white rice. Carbo-loading. When I finished my last bite, I returned to my room to collect my belongings. Then we had a five-minute team meeting at 10:50, during which Coach Schiano gave us a motivational talk. As usual, he was really fired up.

"These guys aren't your friends!" Coach bellowed. "They are out there to win a game just like you, and they are trained to go to war! So you better be ready at all times for anything because they will do anything to win!"

Got it, Coach.

After Coach Schiano was finished inspiring the troops, we boarded the team buses at 11 A.M. for the drive to New Meadowlands Stadium.

I was dressed in a coat and tie—attire that we usually wore for away games. Coach was always big about the spit and polish when we were on the road. "We are the class of college football," he would always say. For home games, though, he wanted us in bright red Rutgers training outfits for the Scarlet Walk, but there was no Scarlet Walk at the Meadowlands. So, even though this was technically a home game for us, Coach Schiano was treating the game like an away contest.

As the buses pulled up to Giants Stadium—that's what I still called the stadium, showing that old habits die hard—I saw all the amazing LED screens affixed to surfaces above the players' entrance. The brilliant jumbo screens were the size of billboards and switched from one digital picture to another. I saw my teammate Antonio Lowery up there about twenty feet tall. He was one of our linebackers, one of our good players, but he was getting the star treatment. *Wow, this is serious*, I thought. *We're going to be playing in Giants Stadium.*

I was excited for another reason: practically all my family was going to be there to watch me play. Normally players get only four complimentary seats, but when you added up the family and friends, I needed about twenty tickets. I got extra seats from out-of-state teammates who weren't using their allotment.

On the family side, Mom was there; my sister, Nicole, and her fiancé, Kenrick Harrigan, and their son, Xavier; Auntie Cheryl and her husband, Uncle Ariel, plus their three kids: Jazmin, Aaron, and James; and my father, Donald McCloud. I appreciated that my dad was there. I didn't see him much, but he was cordial with Mom, so he came with his brother, my Uncle Ricky, and my cousin Jackie Bonafide.

I had old friends from the neighborhood in my box, too. My old Pop Warner coach, Jack Nevins, came with his wife, Sue—the first time she would ever see me play at Rutgers—and their son John. The Liquori family sat in Mom's section, too. I was practically raised on the heavenly pizza from Rocco's Pizzeria, spun from the hands of Rocco Liquori. I grew up playing baseball with his son Alex.

Because of all the friends and family members, Mom went the extra step and hosted a tailgate party in the stadium parking lot before the game. Normally, she hopscotched to other tailgate parties when we played at home, where she hung out with Scott Vallone's parents or Devon Watkins's parents. But this time Uncle Ricky insisted on doing our own tailgate. Some folks brought the hot dogs and hamburgers, others brought the chips and dip, and some brought the beer and soda pop. They did things up right at Mom's tailgate.

Mom left the tailgate early to watch us warm up inside the stadium. Scott Vallone and I had a tradition of taking the field around ninety minutes before kickoff in our "lowers"—pants and cleats—to stretch and limber up. Mom came down to the first row behind the

Rutgers bench and tried to make eye contact with me. We had a little tradition worked out before every game: when our eyes met, she'd point at me, and I would nod my head.

I knew Mom would be out there, so I allowed my eyes to scan the nearly empty seats behind the Rutgers bench. That's when I saw her happy face. When she noticed me looking in her direction, she waved her hand.

I nodded to her, and then I went about my business. I was already locked into the game.

An Early Lead

The New Meadowlands Stadium was about half filled (41,292 attended the game), but it didn't feel that way. Fans occupied the field and mezzanine levels, leaving only the highest deck empty. Most in attendance were Rutgers fans; they were dressed in bright red and fired up to see us play on an NFL field.

My teammates were as keyed up to play in an NFL venue as our hard-core fans. Just before the opening kickoff, our defensive end Sorie Bayoh wielded an axe and ran around our sideline to pump us up. Even though our energy level was high, Army drew first blood with the Black Knights dominating the first half to take a 17–3 lead into the locker room. We only had ourselves to blame: a blocked punt by Army—a special teams play—and a recovery at our 12-yard line led to their first touchdown. Chas Dodd wasn't getting the protection he needed, and we were making too many mistakes and getting hit with too many penalties.

There were some frustrated Scarlet Knights in the locker room at intermission, and Coach Schiano wasn't in a gracious mood. He ripped into us about what we were doing wrong—missed assignments, lazy tackling, and ill-timed penalties. "There's a whole half left, so we can't worry about the fourth quarter now. We have to chop to each individual play one by one," he said.

We kicked off to start the second half. Even though San San Te's kick was short, we held Army's return man Josh Jackson to a 17-yard runback. Then the Black Knights ran their triple option offense to perfection—three, four yards a pop—and advanced to our 24-yard line, with a third-and-four.

Army had rushed the ball down our throats *eleven* straight times, so you might say that I was expecting the run. Trent Steelman handed the ball off to Jared Hassin, and I was in the pile that stopped him for a one-yard gain.

Fourth-and-three from the 23 yard-line. Army was just outside their red zone. I expected the Black Knights to kick a field goal and take the three points, but their coach, Rich Ellerson, waved his offense back on the field. They were going for it. Perhaps Ellerson sensed that if Army made a first down, they'd work their way to the end zone. That would put us in a huge 24–3 hole, which would be a big ask for our young offense.

Then Steelman dropped back to pass! Our linebackers and corners were ready, and his pass fell incomplete.

That was the break we needed. Our offense mounted a *twenty-one*-play drive that took up the rest of the third quarter. I had never had such a long break in my life, sitting on the bench and resting up for the next series of downs.

I stood up, though, when Coach Schiano rolled his own set of dice on fourth down. It was fourth-and-two on Army's 3-yard line, so technically we could still get a first down, but there was no doubt that Coach was going for six points.

Chas rolled to his right and hit Kordell Young in the end zone, and with the extra point, it was a one-score game, 17–10. All the momentum was on our side, and when our well-rested defense got a quick stop, the Scarlet Knights scored the tying touchdown with

5:16 to go on another Chas Dodd touchdown pass, this time to Mark Harrison.

"Kickoff team!" yelled Robb Smith, our special teams coach.

I jogged out on the field, reviewing the instructions my coaches had given me in the pregame meetings. The Army players were very precise and very tough on kickoff returns, which meant I could expect to be double-teamed. They were also aware from game film that I was one of the guys to watch out for.

"Go around to the outside and get right back in your lane," Coach Smith told me. With his advice ringing in my ears, I knew exactly what to do to avoid the double-team. A tackle inside the 20-yard line would pin Army back deep in their own territory.

The time was 4:46 P.M., Eastern Standard Time, on October 16, 2010—a moment that will forever be etched in my mind.

9

THE COLLISION

Up in the broadcast booth, Bob Picozzi was calling the play-by-play for ESPN3, which streamed the game live on the Internet on pay-per-view.

It's late in the fourth quarter. Tie game. So we have a new football game with 5:16 left.

I knew the Army receiving unit would have two guys waiting for me. They had been throwing a double-team at me on every kick-off, and this was the fourth of the afternoon.

San San Te to kick off. This is a good one.

This time, the Black Knights had Malcolm Brown, a talented and fast slot back, back deep. Their regular returner, Josh Jackson, hadn't had a good day against us, so maybe Brown would give them a spark.

I was in a full sprint as San San Te's kickoff settled into the arms of the Army kick returner a few yards inside the goal line. He was on my side of the field. In fact, if you drew a straight line between us, I had a direct beeline on him. There were 35 yards between us, but we were each running at full speed, so the distance was closing fast.

Inside the five. It's Malcolm Brown . . .

I was getting excited because the play was coming straight at me. I knew where I wanted to hit him. I was going to throw my shoulder right into his chest. As the distance closed between us, I remembered to set up my body.

His lead blockers were starting to pick up our people as the gap between us narrowed. Just as I expected, two guys tried to slow me down, but I made a quick juking move and slipped past them. In a split second, I saw Brown right in front of me. I had a clear shot.

Instinct took over. Just before I exploded into him, one of my teammates dove for his legs. Brown responded by swiveling his hips and twisting ever so slightly as he reached the impact zone.

I was set to throw my shoulder into his midsection—the classic "bite the ball" way to tackle—but Brown had been spun a bit. Instead of hitting him in the chest with my shoulder—where I was aiming—my helmet rammed into the back of his left shoulder, striking his collarbone. The collision between helmet and bone made a sickening sound that ricocheted through the stadium. It all happened in tenths of a second.

Oooh! What a great open-field hit by Eric LeGrand, who was shaken up by the play . . .

When I nailed him, my body instantly went stiff, and I felt like I was in a movie. My vision immediately blurred, and everything slowed down. I immediately fell to the ground like a giant oak that had been cut down, landing on my back.

Two enterprising reporters with the *Star-Ledger*, Jackie Friedman and Frank Cecala, calculated the forces at play at the moment of collision. They estimated that I was moving at 6.4 yards per second, or 13.18 miles per hour, down the field. Malcolm Brown had ignited his afterburner after catching the kickoff: he was moving at a clip of 10 yards per second, or 20.45 mph.

I hit him really hard. The gruesome crash exerted 833 pounds of force on each of us, which the *Star-Ledger* reported would be the same as a 150-pound world-class sprinter running at top speed into a brick wall. It was the "perfect storm of size, speed, and catastrophic misfortune," wrote Friedman and Cecala.

If you watch the replay on YouTube—which I have numerous times—the crowd makes an immediate *oooh* after we collided. That's how the loud the sound of impact was. If my head was just a few more degrees upright, I would have gotten up, dusted myself off, and gone about my business. But as it happened, the colossal impact between the tip of my helmet and the thin padding covering Malcolm's collarbone resulted in my spinal cord taking the full impact of the crushing blow.

My body involuntarily stiffened as the nerve stem between my brain and the rest of my body instantly blacked out—as if a power switch had been turned off. I spun through the air and landed flat on my back, unable to move. The last thing I felt were my legs going down to the ground. My body went *ding,* and a loud ringing sound swirled through my brain.

I knew something bad had happened. Really bad. Just how horrible, I didn't know, but this was way beyond any hits I had received or dished out on the football field.

The wallop sent Malcolm Brown sprawling to the turf, and I'm sure he felt an immediate sharp pain from the fracture of his collarbone. He was quickly helped to his feet and assisted off the field by his teammates, holding his left shoulder with his right arm.

Of course, I knew nothing about what was happening to the Army kick returner. What I recall is the instantaneous sensation of feeling stiff—as if I were experiencing rigor mortis—while I fell ever-so-slowly through the air and landed on my back. I couldn't do anything to break my fall.

Once I hit the ground, though, adrenaline surged through my body. *You gotta get up! Get up!* I had always pushed myself to my knees and gotten up after being knocked down—ever since I was a first grader when Charlie Schwartz sent me flying into the basketball pole.

This time, however, I couldn't move anything—my legs, my arms, or my torso. I tried pulling myself off the ground again, but nothing happened. I could move my head slightly, but that was about it.

Must be a legit full stinger, I thought. A stinger is a neurological injury that athletes in high-contact sports like football, rugby, or ice hockey sometimes experience. A nerve in the spine or neck gets pinched from contact, and the result is a stinging sensation in the affected area. But I couldn't feel any part of my body stinging, so it couldn't be that.

Two teammates, defensive backs Duron Harmon and Patrick Kivlehan, came over to see how I was doing—but they immediately stepped back. A couple of other teammates also determined that something didn't look right. They looked over to our sideline and made a waving motion, but our trainers were already on the run. Coach Schiano was fast on their heels.

I looked out through my mask and kept still. I quickly realized I was out of breath and needed air. I gasped and tried to say the words *I can't breathe* to anyone who could hear me, but I couldn't press out the air necessary to form the words in my larynx.

Two Rutgers trainers, a bit winded from the long sprint, came into my vision and knelt beside me.

"Is it your head or your neck?" asked one in a frantic voice.

I can't breathe!

At least, that's what I wanted to say, but the words wouldn't come out. I tried to mouth the thought, but with my helmet still on, my trainers couldn't read my lips.

"Can you feel me touching your hand?" asked the other trainer.

I didn't answer. I couldn't move. I couldn't breathe.

"Head or neck!" yelled the first trainer, the panic rising in his voice.

Once again, I couldn't form the words.

"Head or neck, Eric!" he repeated.

My eyes bulged in fear. I was panicking myself. I thought I was going to run out of air any second and die. They had to do something to help me!

I tried to mouth the words *I can't breathe, I can't breathe*, but I wasn't having any success.

Coach Schiano leaned into my view. He was on his knees with a furrowed brow. Coach looked as concerned as I had ever seen him. When he had sprinted across the field, he shot a quick prayer heavenward: *Please, Lord, just let him be knocked out.*

"Eric, you just got to pray," he said to me. "Just pray that you're going to be fine."

I can't breathe, Coach. I can't breathe. This time I rasped some of the sounds, but Coach and no one else could understand what I was trying to get across. What I didn't know at the time was that when I severely injured my spinal cord, there was an immediate loss of nerve supply to the entire body, including my heart and blood vessels. A sudden and profound drop in blood pressure occurred, which is known as "spinal shock."

I sensed urgency from the next wave of responders who surrounded me, but I also heard the voices of other players:

He's probably got a concussion. He'll be fine.

No, I saw him fall. I don't like the way he hit the ground.

I hope he'll be okay.

It's bad, man.

In the stadium, a quiet murmur fell over the crowd. Mom was sitting in a lower field-level section on the 25-yard line with a direct view of the collision. She was becoming more panicked by the second. Mom stood next to my sister, Nicole, who was next to her fiancé, Kenny. On Mom's right side was Sue Nevins. Everyone close to me was there to cheer me on to victory. Now they all looked on in horror as I lay motionless on the field.

"Don't worry," said Mrs. Nevins, trying to be helpful. "He's going to be okay."

Something about the way I fell didn't sit right with Mom. She had seen me get knocked on my butt hundreds of times—but never like this. Every time in every other game, I had immediately risen to my feet. But there was something grotesquely different to what she had just witnessed, and it was the way I fell to the ground and bounced on the turf like I was a teeter-totter. My legs, which were raised off the ground, had gone stiff as a board.

Her heart was in her throat as she watched Coach Schiano, trainers, and medical staff form a circle around me. A white cart marked EMS zoomed across the field. It was at the moment that the situation went from *Oh-my-God-what-happened?* to *This-could-be-really-serious.*

Everyone was mute around her, mirroring the hushed silence inside the cavernous stadium. Mom scanned the field, trying to process information. Every player on the Rutgers and Army teams had taken a knee. Some bowed their heads in prayer and didn't care who knew. Others had pensive looks of disbelief at what was happening. All were grim-faced and silent. Tears began forming in Mom's eyes and rolled down her face. She knew something really, really bad had happened to me.

Mom suddenly saw a distressed man in a Rutgers windbreaker running in her direction, waving for her to come on the field. He was part of Coach Schiano's security detail, and Coach had told him to make sure that he got my mom.

"Ms. LeGrand? Can you come with me?"

My mother didn't hesitate to gather her purse and light jacket. She had to be with her baby.

"You want to come?" she asked Nicole.

"I'm coming," my sister responded.

Mom and Nicole stepped down the aisle, and the security staffer assisted them onto the field. They watched from afar as nearly a dozen medical personnel and trainers gingerly set me on a hard plastic backboard.

Mom saw all sorts of people working me as I lay on the ground, totally helpless. And that's how she felt at that moment: totally helpless and unable to do anything. She wanted me to see her face, to let me know that Mom was there, to hold on and know that everything was going to be okay.

Mom held Nicole close and prayed that I would be okay. She wore a scarlet Rutgers jersey over a T-shirt, emblazoned with the number 52 on the front and back. Across the back of my mother's shoulders were these two words:

LeGrand's Mom

What Was Going On?

Sometimes people who have been put in incredibly stressful situations—such as major trauma—will say they felt a sense of peace during the moment of the injury. They'll describe how everything slowed down, allowing them time to grasp their new reality with greater clarity.

But I wasn't feeling any sense of peace. I was in a fight for my life. I feared the worst, that this might have been my time to leave this earth, and I fought to hold on to the next minute, the next breath.

I heard Coach Schiano's voice. "Slow down," he said, "Slow everything down. You're going to be fine, but just keep on praying."

I didn't pray, not right then. I was too busy trying to breathe. A few moments later, however, I did think to ask: *God, what is going on?*

It seemed like a logical question. Even though I hadn't gone to church much growing up, I certainly believed in God and his Son, Jesus Christ. This seemed like one of those foxhole moments to ask a question like that, but I didn't get an answer. So I prayed some more. My mind pleaded with the Almighty that I would be all right.

God, please let me catch my breath.

God, please let me get up.

God, please let me move.

God, what is going on?

Six or seven emergency personnel took a few moments to gingerly lift me atop the backboard and securely fasten me. Then our director of player services, Mike Kuzniak, unfastened the face mask attached to my helmet. Kuz removed the T-nuts and screws in record time.

Next, the Rutgers team physician, Dr. Robert Monaco, gave me a shot, jabbing my leg with a syringe. The medicine was supposed to reduce the initial inflammation and boost my chances of overcoming a spinal cord injury, but it had to be administered within five to ten minutes of the injury.

Once the responders were satisfied that I was stable and immobilized—which included taping my helmeted head to the backboard—eight or nine men lifted me up and placed me on the bed of the EMS cart. The act of lifting me off the ground gave me a gasp of much-needed air.

But just a gasp. I did feel a little better, but that was momentary. I started panting in an attempt to draw enough air into my lungs.

As the driver swung the cart around to take me off the field, I heard the public address announcer say, "Eric LeGrand."

Thousands of fans clapped respectfully. Because of the subdued, polite applause, I desperately wanted to give the crowd a thumbs-up from my prone position on the cart—to let them know I would be all right. That should be simple enough—raising my hand with thumb extended into the air.

But I couldn't move any of my fingers. It felt like there was a thousand pounds holding my thumb down. As I lay on the backboard, I wanted to look at my right hand, thinking that if I could somehow see my fingers, then my hand would move the thumb on my command. But I was immobilized, and my entire right arm remained limp.

This is so weird. Maybe my body was in shock—and that's why I couldn't move a muscle. I kept trying and trying, but nothing worked. I had shaken off so many injuries in the past, but this was something I had never experienced before.

Meanwhile, broadcaster Bob Picozzi of ESPN3 was adding his thoughts to the story unfolding on the field. "Our thoughts and prayers, needless to say, are with Eric and his family," Picozzi said. "It's always disconcerting when you see something like this happen, when you judge what the immediate observations are from the others around it, and you saw Greg Schiano come flying across the field. In fact, Greg is on the far sideline, and I wonder whether he is talking to a family member."

The broadcast switched to a visual of Coach Schiano speaking with Mom and Nicole. He placed both arms on Mom's shoulders and locked eyes with her while Nicole looked on. Coach had always believed in the personal touch.

"Just pray," were his words. "Just pray."

Mom swallowed. She tried her best to gather herself, but she wasn't succeeding. Tears flowed once again. Then Mom whispered another prayer: *Please, God, don't take him away from me.*

Coach directed Mom and Nicole to the tunnel where we came out onto the field, where a paramedic's van would be waiting for me. As Mom walked, she prayed for the strength to get through whatever was going to happen.

The EMT cart pulled into the tunnel shielded from public view. Team officials escorted Mom and Nicole to my side.

When I saw my mother, she looked scared. I summoned the strength to say, "I'm going to be okay, Mom," but I garbled the words and my voice was barely above a whisper.

Mom says that she saw panic in my eyes. Because I looked scared, she was scared. All her life she had looked out for me, paved the path, fulfilled my every need, but now life had sent me in a totally different direction, and she was totally helpless to do anything about it.

My spirits sank as the seriousness of my situation became more pronounced. I couldn't move, could barely breathe, and couldn't feel anything. My mind was starting to freak out from the gravity of the situation, and I momentarily blacked out. When I woke up an instant later, everything was blurry around me. The spinal shock was causing my blood pressure to drop precipitously.

I was rolled into an ambulance on a gurney, and everyone seemed to know what they were doing. Playing in an NFL stadium helped; the emergency responders were prepared to deal with these types of injuries and had tons of experience. One of the EMTs directed Mom to get into the front seat, while Nicole said she was running out to the parking lot. She would follow in her car.

I remembered something. "Mom," I whispered.

My mother leaned closer from her passenger seat.

"Call Rheanne," I said. I wanted Mom to reach my girlfriend

and let her know that I would be all right. She was back in New Brunswick, watching the game on her computer.

A paramedic placed an oxygen mask over my mouth and nose. I was surprised that the mask didn't help as much as I thought it would. I would have loved a lot more air filling my lungs, but then I blacked out before we left the stadium.

Nicole told me later there was no siren as we pulled away. The ambulance did not speed to the hospital. She didn't know where we were going, of course, but the ambulance drove at normal speed limits and moved cautiously through intersections. Because the EMTs thought I had suffered a potentially paralyzing injury, they were trying to minimize any jarring to my neck that I might feel from bumps in the road.

I do remember being aware of arriving at the hospital in an enclosed garagelike building, although everything was blurry. I heard all sorts of echoes as I was unloaded from the van and quickly wheeled through open doors. Awaiting me was Mom with Nicole. I was taken to some type of emergency room, where I heard a sound of *boom-boom, boom-boom*. I had no idea what it was. The lights were bright as people fluttered about me, moving quickly.

From that point until basically the following Wednesday, I barely remember anything at all, but Mom has since filled me in on all the activity and commotion that happened while I was in and out of a deep semicoma.

I had been taken to the Hackensack University Medical Center in Hackensack, New Jersey, five miles away from the Meadowlands. A half-dozen tight-lipped doctors took turns examining me, but they weren't saying anything. The first thing they had to do was take my helmet off, which was something they wanted to do *very carefully* since they knew that at the very least I had suffered some type of neck injury. They took their time prying the tight helmet from my head, which was covered by a red skullcap from Nike. My dreadlocks had been bunched up inside the tight cap before I slipped on my helmet.

I don't know how long that took, but around forty-five minutes after my arrival, Dr. Roy Vingan walked into the waiting room, where Mom, tons of family members, teammates like Scott Vallone and his family, and old friends from Avenel like Nate Brown and Brandon Hall had gathered. The neurosurgeon pulled my mother aside with a touch of her elbow.

"Eric cannot move," he said. "He has broken his neck and needs surgery." He further explained that the collision had cracked two vertebrae near the top of my spinal column—the C3 and the C4. "Right now, he cannot move his arms or legs."

Mom was in a daze. She didn't know what to say. Her mind was not ready to go to the word *paralyzed*. Not yet. Not while there was so much up in the air.

The doctor cleared his throat. "We do not know when your son will be able to move," he continued, as if he was reading her mind. "We will have to wait until after surgery. We know that the first seventy-two hours after surgery are the most critical. It's important that he have some feeling or movement within that time period."

"Will he . . . will he be all right?" my mom managed.

"We don't know," the doctor replied. "We will be attempting to repair what we can during surgery. And then we have to wait and see. Seventy-two hours is key. Before we start, you can go see him."

My mom's eyes brightened. I'm told that I was awake, but I don't remember seeing Mom before I went into surgery. Even though my helmet had been removed, I was still wearing my entire football uniform.

Mom wanted to lean forward to kiss me, but she couldn't. She had been cautioned not to touch me due to my dire condition.

Unable to pat the son she loved, another wave of tears flooded out like a dam that been breached.

"You're going to be okay," she whispered. "You're going to be okay. The doctors say you have to have surgery, so be brave. I'm here for you. I love you."

My eyes were open, and Mom says I looked at her, but I didn't know who she was. In fact, I had no idea what was happening. I saw forms moving around, but I couldn't figure out what I was doing there.

The following morning, many hours later, Mom was handed a large plastic bag containing my helmet, pads, jersey, socks, and jock strap; my clothing had been cut into strips to remove it from my body.

That plastic bag is somewhere in storage today. I'm sure I'll check out the contents of that bag some time, but that won't be difficult for me. What's difficult is thinking back to that moment when everything changed in an instant—and knowing the hardship my injury placed on my mom and my family.

Looking for the Best

When Mom returned to the waiting room, Coach Schiano was pacing about, a cell phone glued to his ear. He continued to speak with someone, and as soon as he was finished with one call, he was on to the next.

Coach was calling everyone he knew to make sure this was the best place for me to be. He was asking questions like:

Is Hackensack okay?

Should Eric be going somewhere else?

Should we be flying him to another hospital?

His immediate concern was my welfare. The Giants trainer told my coach that I was in the best place possible. "Hackensack is a Trauma 1 place," the trainer said. "That's where we send all our players with this sort of injury, so he's in the best spot. Dr. Vingan is an excellent neurosurgeon."

A nurse called Mom over to her station. There were all sorts of consent papers that she had to sign on my behalf. Each noted the profound risk involved with surgery on a broken neck and specifically spelled out the possibility that I might not survive the trip to the operating table. Once the paperwork was done, the vigil started for the two dozen or so people in the waiting room.

My operation began around 8 P.M. on Saturday. For the next nine hours, a group of doctors performed delicate decompression surgery to stabilize my spine. The reason the operation took so long is that they had to align my broken neck in such a way that I would be able to breathe and swallow in the future. What many people don't realize is that if a broken neck heals in a zigzag fashion, the patient will have difficulty breathing and swallowing for the rest of his or her life.

Few if any of those in the hospital waiting room vigil slept a wink. Coach Schiano sat in a chair and propped his feet on another chair to rest his eyelids.

Hours earlier, Coach had presided over a somber postgame press conference, even though we had beaten Army 23–20 in overtime. Gripping the podium tightly and biting his lip, Coach leaned forward and made an opening statement to the assembled reporters and news cameras.

"Let me start with Eric LeGrand," he said. "He has been taken to Hackensack Medical Center. If I could ask you—and I know it's your job—but if we could respect his family and his privacy right now, it would mean a lot to me and to his family. As soon as it is appropriate, I will get word to you. I promise.

"It's all tough stuff. When you coach these kids, they're your kids. That's the thing that I don't know if everyone gets. It's not pro football. Those are your kids. You're raising them and finishing the job of the parents, so it's tough."

The pain clearly registered on his face. He answered several football questions professionally and perfunctorily, and then he excused himself, saying he wanted to get over to the hospital.

Little did Coach Schiano know, the win over Army would be our last victory of the 2010 season. Rutgers would go on to lose six consecutive games, unable to overcome a black cloud that settled over the program when Malcolm Brown and I crashed into each other like runaway freight trains.

Coming Out of Surgery

Throughout the long night at Hackensack, Mom worked a handkerchief, dabbing her eyes from the tears. Her prayer was that I would make it through surgery somehow. As the hours passed by, though, many could not keep their eyes open any longer. My sister Nicole would fall asleep and wake up, then fall asleep and wake up again. Coach Schiano was knocked out—mouth wide open and snoring away.

At five in the morning, when it was still pitch dark outside, Dr. Vingan startled the dazed crowd with his entrance. Sleeping bodies stirred in the waiting room. Once again he pulled my mother aside.

"I'm sorry for taking so long," he began, as if he needed to apologize. "We never expected the surgery to take as long as it did. First of all, Eric is stable. The reason everything took so long is that we operated on the front of his neck, and then we had to flip him over to do some things in the back of his neck. We were not happy with the initial results, so we had to redo some things. It's important that his spinal column line up."

Screws were used to help set my spinal cord straight. "We see many patients where their spinal cords zigzag, but Eric's spinal column looks perfectly straight to us. This is paramount in terms of him being able to swallow."

This was a lot of information for Mom to take in. *Swallow? What about walking again?* But she wasn't prepared to go there with the doctor.

"I cannot overemphasize the importance of the first seventy-two hours," he said. "Our hope is that we will see movement during that time as we await for the swelling in the spine to subside. The issue is more about the level of the injury on the spine than the completeness of the injury."

Dr. Vingan took his time to explain that the spinal cord does not have to be severed to cause paralysis. The spinal cord carries electrical impulses from the brain through a jellylike tube of neural tissues out to the extremities and back again. Protecting this soft tube of neural tissues is a spinal column made up of thirty-three bones, or vertebrae. Cervical vertebra at the topmost portion of the spine are numbered 1 through 8. The higher the injury on the spinal column, the closer the injury is to the brain. The closer to the brain, the more likely the injury will affect your ability to move your arms and legs and have feeling.

"Eric's injury happened to the C3 and C4 vertebrae, which is quite high," Dr. Vingan said. "We estimate that Eric has a zero to five percent chance of regaining neurologic function."

"That low?" Mom didn't like hearing that.

"I'm afraid so, Ms. LeGrand."

She decided that she didn't want any doctors talking to me. She didn't want me to know what the medical experts thought about my chances. She wanted me to stay positive. She hadn't given up hope. Mom believed in me, and she would help me fight through this.

On Sunday evening, Mom and Rheanne were in the intensive care unit. In my semiconscious state, I sensed I had visitors.

And then I remembered something—*practice*. I had to get to practice.

"I gotta go," I whispered. "Coach doesn't like it if we're late to practice."

Keep in mind that I was flat on my back, barely able to utter these words because of all the tubes down my throat.

"It's okay, Eric," Rheanne soothed. "You don't have to go to practice today," fighting back tears.

"Did you win today?"

For some reason, I had correctly remembered that the women's soccer team had a game on Sunday afternoon.

"No, we tied St. John's, but I played well." What Rheanne didn't say was that her coach took her out after the first half because he could see that she was clearly not herself. She didn't include that information because she didn't want me to worry about her.

Later that evening, several close friends were allowed to see me: Tyler Jackow, Brandon Hall, and Joey LaSala. Once again I mouthed a question that was barely above a whisper: "Hey, guys, what are we doing tonight?"

"E, I think you just need to chill for the night," Tyler said.

I must have repeated the question three times. We continued trying to have a conversation, but one by one, the guys would excuse themselves to step outside of my ICU room. And that's where they'd break down and sob out of my earshot.

I had no idea that people were crying after seeing me. Every time somebody came into my room, it was all positive energy:

It's going to be all right, Eric.

Everything is going to be fine.

You'll be playing football in no time.

But the kicker of that Sunday evening was when Coach Schiano stepped into my room. He expressed love and concern for me, but I interrupted him with a random question that I couldn't get out of my mind. "Coach, there's one thing I always wanted to ask you. Do you think I can play in the NFL?"

Coach Schiano never blinked an eye. "Your chances are as good as anyone else's," he said. But after he answered me, he had to bite his lip again to hold back the tears.

Mom and Coach Schiano stepped into the hallway. There were decisions that had to be made regarding the press. Dozens of reporters had swarmed Hackensack Medical Center, waiting to report an update on my condition. Satellite trucks ringed the hospital. The media—television, print, and Internet—were reporting that I had "sustained a neck injury" and was taken to Hackensack. ESPN and New York and New Jersey local news shows replayed the video clip of my collision with Malcolm Brown over and over again, and each time I failed to move a muscle after I went down. Nobody was saying it, but the unspoken question on everyone's mind was: *Is he paralyzed?*

The chances of becoming paralyzed while playing in an organized football game are very, very low—but it happens in our sport. Football is a game of bodies crashing into each other, a full-contact sport where the rate of injury is considerably higher than say, baseball or tennis. Usually the major injuries are torn-up knees or concussions. Around forty thousand concussions are recorded each year at the high school level, according to the Brain Injury Association, and knee injuries have to be much more common.

According to the 2009 Annual Survey of Catastrophic Football Injuries, seven cervical cord injuries with incomplete neurological recovery occurred to football players at the high school level and one at the college level. This would make the rate of this type of serious injury 0.46 and 1.33 per 100,000 players, respectively.

The chances of becoming a quadriplegic and being paralyzed from the neck down are even more remote. This type of injury seems to happen every twenty-five years or so in the college game. On October 26, 1985, Marc Buoniconti, the son of Hall of Fame linebacker Nick Buoniconti of the Miami Dolphins, hurtled headfirst into an upended runner while playing for The Citadel. Buoniconti instantly fell to the ground limp, paralyzed. He has been confined to a wheelchair without movement in his arms or legs ever since. Before Buoniconti's time, you'd have to go back to 1970, when Cornell football player Ken Kunken broke his neck, leaving him almost totally paralyzed from the shoulders down.

A couple of NFL players have left the field unable to walk again. Perhaps the best-known case happened before my time during an NFL preseason game in 1978. New England Patriots wide receiver Darryl Stingley was crossing the field and leaped up to haul in a pass. Jack Tatum of the Oakland Raiders absolutely destroyed the defenseless receiver, fracturing his C4 and C5 vertebrae and rendering Stingley a quadriplegic for the rest of his life. He was only able to regain very limited movement in his right arm, and the NFL changed its rules to curtail aggressive plays. Darryl Stingley died in 2007 at the age of fifty-five.

The other notable injury was during the 1991 season. Mike Utley, a right guard with the Detroit Lions, fractured his C6 and C7 vertebrae, but he has complete use of his upper extremities, making him a paraplegic.

Of course, there are also those who beat the odds. Kevin Everett, whose story sounded eerily like mine, was a tight end who saw a lot of special teams play for the Buffalo Bills during the 2007 NFL season. While attempting to tackle Denver Bronco player Domenik Hixon on a kickoff return, Kevin sustained a severe, life-threatening cervical spine injury to his C3 and C4 vertebrae. He was told that he'd probably never regain the use of arms and legs.

But he did, crediting his faith in God and his rehab.

The other miracle comeback belonged to Penn State cornerback Adam Taliaferro, who suffered a career-ending spinal cord injury in 2000, but he had made a miraculous recovery to walk his team onto the field a year later.

Coach Schiano reached out to Adam Taliaferro's father in the hours following my accident. Coach, who knew the Taliaferro family because he had been the defensive backs coach at Penn State in the 1990s, asked Adam's father what my family could expect after suffering a spinal cord injury.

He learned that it would be a long, tough road ahead. While Penn State had some experience with this sort of catastrophic injury, my situation was entirely new for the Rutgers football program. Both Coach and Mom agreed that the task of dealing with the press should remain with our Sports Information Department.

On Sunday evening, Rutgers released new information about my condition, and for the first time, the P-word was officially employed when the team announced that I was paralyzed from the neck down. "Eric's spirits were as good as you can expect," Coach Schiano was quoted as saying. "He was cognizant of me being there, his mom, everybody. He's a fighter."

No doubt thinking about Adam Taliaferro, Coach said, "We're going to believe Eric LeGrand is going to walk onto that field with us. That's what we will believe."

Believe.

I had always liked that word.

10

THE SEVENTY-TWO-HOUR WINDOW

I had no idea what was being said or written about me during the first few days after my catastrophic injury. I didn't know anything about the "seventy-two-hour window," nor was I aware that my Rutgers teammates showed their support by having stickers attached to the front of their helmets. Their one-word message to the world: BELIEVE.

All this was happening outside my hospital room, a world that seemed like a million miles away. I had more important things on my mind, like when I would regain use of my limbs. I thought feelings and sensation would return any moment—or that I'd wake up from this bad dream. My spirits remained high as my new reality set in, partially because I truly believed I would walk again. I figured all I needed was a double dose of patience and time to allow my body to rebound from such a massive hit.

I really don't remember anything before Wednesday, when I recall Mom bending over me, her sad eyes looking into mine. I was uncomfortable with a breathing tube down my throat as well as a feeding tube. Monitors filled the ICU with white noise.

Relief washed over me. Mom was there at my darkest hour.

"I'll be back," I croaked.

"Yes, you'll surprise everyone," she said.

But then we received a wallop of bad news that Wednesday afternoon. Mom told me that my doctors were greatly concerned about my ability to breathe. They wanted to cut a hole into my windpipe, or trachea, and insert a tube that was connected to a ventilator to supply oxygen to my lungs. A decision was made to wait for twenty-four hours.

On Thursday, my doctors felt that they could delay the operation no longer. That afternoon, I was wheeled once again into the operating room, where I underwent a tracheotomy procedure. Afterward, my medical team told Mom that I would likely never breathe on my own and would always need a ventilator.

After the tracheotomy, I heard familiar voices speaking—Mom and Rheanne. I tried to get their attention by clucking my tongue.

Rheanne drew close. "Yes! I'm here!"

"Will you help me walk again?" I managed to press out.

She flashed that great smile of hers. "Yes, I will help you walk again."

Hearing that, my thought was, *Good, we got this.*

The ventilator made it difficult to communicate. Normally when I spoke or tried to make a sound, air passed through the larynx. When the ventilator was put in place, however, most of the air bypassed my voice box. A small amount got around the ventilator tube, though, and allowed me to whisper a few words before I ran out of breath.

I quickly lost tolerance for the machine that assisted my breathing. The thing itched like crazy and made a terrible racket each time the ventilator inhaled and exhaled for me. The noise made sleep impossible. I was also worried that the ventilator tube would fall out and no one would be around to connect the apparatus to the

This is me with Nana, my term of endearment for my grandmother, Betty LeGrand.

My sister, Nicole, is eleven years older than me, but when I was a kindergartner, I thought we were the same age.

During my early years, we lived in an apartment complex in Woodbridge, New Jersey, where Mom set up this backyard pool. I liked to splash Nicole when she wasn't looking.

If a toy had wheels, I was on it. I loved riding my battery-operated "motorcycle" up and down the sidewalks in Woodbridge.

I was crazy about Batman. Here I'm getting ready to do some trick or treating on Halloween as the Caped Crusader.

I was an energetic kid, so Mom signed me up for Pop Warner football. I was six years old when this photo was taken—my last season of flag football.

This was my first year of tackle football—at the age of seven. Mom used to stand on the sidelines to watch my games, and whenever I turned the corner with the goal line in sight, she'd run with me toward the end zone.

When I was ten years old, I moved up to the Pee Wee division because of my weight. Most of my teammates were at least a year older than me.

My most memorable childhood vacation was a Caribbean cruise with Mom, Nicole, Nana, and Auntie Cheryl. Everything was great except for the time they left me behind at the ship's camp for kids, while they went onshore and had fun.

Even though I don't look too interested here, I loved playing baseball. When I was twelve, I was part of our area All-Star Little League team, and we made a serious run at the Little League World Series in Williamsport, Pennsylvania.

I wore No. 30 throughout most of my Pop Warner days and while playing high school football at Colonia High. Denver Bronco running back Terrell Davis, my idol growing up, had the same number. I was in seventh grade when this picture was taken.

I played one year of high school baseball. I pitched, but I had control problems and once plunked three hitters from South River.

I got called up from the freshman team to play the last three varsity games of the season. I played so well—forty-five tackles in three games—that I was eventually offered a scholarship to play football at Rutgers University.

Posing by the field house at Colonia High with my mom after one of my football games during senior year.

I loved everything about football—even the warm up. The excitement and anticipation of playing a game before thousands of fans as a Scarlet Knight is a feeling I'll never forget.

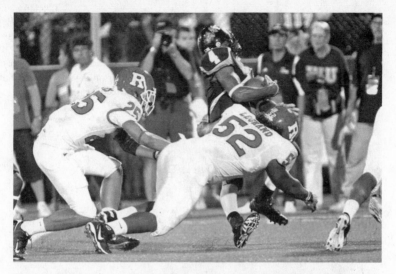

Here I am making a textbook tackle, leading with my shoulder and wrapping up the runner to drive him to the ground.

I was part of the kickoff and kickoff return teams at Rutgers. I loved sprinting down the field on a kickoff play and making big tackles inside the twenty-yard line.

Football is a game of emotion, and you truly feel like you are going into battle when you run out onto the field. Here I'm lifting a teamate after he made a great play.

I have some great occupational therapists at Kessler, and Sean McCarthy is one of my favorites. Here I'm hooked up to electrical stimulation devices a couple of months after my injury.

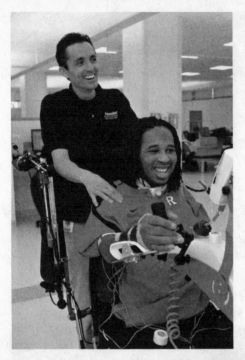

My lovely girlfriend, Rheanne Sleiman, and I started dating five months before my injury in October 2010. Here we are in my room at the Kessler Institute for Rehabilitation in West Orange, New Jersey.

One week after my injury, the Rutgers football team played the University of Pittsburgh, where the Pitt fans showed their support for me.

My Rutgers teammates have stood by me and supported me throughout my recovery, telling me I will walk one day.

I have a great team behind me, from Rheanne to my cousins, Jazmin, Aaron, and James *(on my left),* and my Auntie Cheryl and Uncle Ariel *(next to Mom).* David Tyree, the Super Bowl hero who made the famous "helmet catch" in 2008, is directly behind me along with other members of Team Believe who participated in a Tough Mudder obstacle course to raise funds on my behalf.

Sharing my love for baseball with my nephews, Xavier and Isaac, at the Somerset Patriots minor league ballpark in Bridgewater, New Jersey.

Another great moment was visiting with several New York Mets players at Citi Field. That's Jose Reyes *(far left),* who's now playing for the Miami Marlins, and several of my buddies: Ryan Don Diego, Brandon Hall, Drew Krupinski, and Evan Nadjavestky.

During my locomotor training program, I'm positioned on a treadmill and held in place with a harness. Physical therapists move my legs to help me "walk."

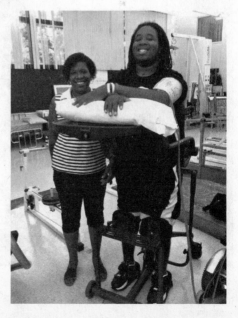

When I stood with the assistance of this special metalized frame at Kessler in the summer of 2011, I tweeted this message: "Standing tall, we can't fall."

Mom is caregiver No. 1, always on call, always there for me.

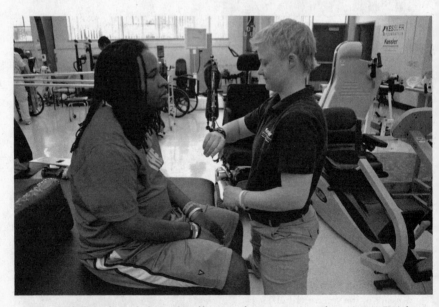

I can't believe how dedicated Buffy, one of my outpatient therapists at Kessler, has been to my recovery. She is always pushing me during our sessions.

These days I can't wait to get into my rehab at Kessler. Here, a technician is putting on my walking shoes before I step onto the NeuroRecovery Network locomotor treadmill.

My team of dedicated therapists at the Kessler Institute of Rehabliltation. Sitting next to me is Buffy, and in the row behind me *(left to right)* are Sydney, Roxanne, Lindsay, Proshud, and Jared.

Having a VW Routan handicap-accessible van has greatly improved the quality of my life. I can go so many places with Mom, family, or friends behind the wheel. I can even get myself in and out of the van using my mouthpiece.

What an awesome guy! I got a chance to meet Tim Tebow at the end of the 2011 season at a home game in Denver, and he couldn't have been nicer—and his team had lost that day! Now he's playing in my backyard as a New York Jet.

Making the pilgrimage to Yankee Stadium in the Bronx, where I chatted with future Hall of Fame shortstop Derek Jeter, one of my favorite ballplayers growing up. That's my nephew Xavier hanging with us.

My sister, Nicole, married Kenrick Harrigan a week before Christmas in 2011. I love having Kenny as a brother-in-law. He's always joking around and is so positive. He really fits in well with our family.

I've received more than a dozen signed footballs wishing me the very best. Each and every football encourages me to keep believing that I will someday walk again.

The encouraging verse from Philippians 4:13 says it all: I can do all things through Christ who strengthens me.

That's me on the red carpet! I made my first trip to the West Coast in June 2012 when I received the first-ever Guysman Trophy for being the "manliest of men" at the Spike TV awards show. It was fun making my way down the red carpet with other sports and Hollywood celebrities.

The picture says it all—and is just a fraction of the support I have received since my injury. Words will never be able to completely express my deep appreciation for the way people have reached out to me with so much love and encouragement.

opening of my windpipe. If that happened, I'd die a slow, horrible death from suffocation.

At the time, I wasn't aware that ventilators routinely come loose or fall out, or that anyone with caregiving experience can rapidly insert the tube into the tracheotomy, so it was extra frightening a day or two later when I had my first ventilator episode. Rheanne was in the room and dishing about stuff happening on campus and the latest news regarding the women's soccer team. She also described the amazing amount of support of the Rutgers students and all around the tri-state area. I tried to take a deep breath, and more air got through than I expected. Result: the ventilator came loose.

No nurse was in the room or in the hallways. The unconnected vent set off all sorts of alarms. Rheanne panicked because she didn't know what to do. I couldn't help her, of course, and the sudden cutoff of fresh-flowing oxygen caused me to panic. I breathed as deeply as I could through my nose while precious seconds passed. No nurses responded to the alarms that had been set off.

Rheanne had to do some quick thinking while I breathed through my nose like there was no tomorrow.

"Let me try this," she said.

Rheanne shoved her thumb into the hole in my windpipe in an attempt to stop the wheezing until she could put the tube back into my throat.

"Can you breathe now?" she asked.

My lungs expanded with the inflow of air, and my panic subsided. I nodded my head to signal that air was coming through the vent again.

That incident certainly gave the both of us a scare, and I wish I could say that the next time my tube fell out I would take everything in stride. But that was never the case. I could not wait to get off the ventilator, but I had no idea at the time if that was even going to be a possibility.

As for regaining movement in my arms and legs or experiencing any sensation below my neck, nothing was happening on that
front. My mom and Rutgers University decided to let the important
seventy-two-hour marker pass without commenting publicly on my
condition.

These were the first few days of the rest of my life. Now that
I was gaining an awareness of my surroundings, I couldn't get my
head around what happened. I didn't accept the enormity of my
injury—at least not yet. I mean, I knew I had received a horrible
neck fracture on the football field. I also understood that I would
never have the same life as before, but that's about as far as I got in
my thinking.

Most of the time, my thoughts were more immediate: How
could I get through the next minute, the next hour? Was life always
going to be like this? Would I ever move my arms again or go for a
simple walk on a tree-shaded path?

The uncertainty about the road ahead was why I was afraid of
being left alone—and wanted Mom with me all the time. She stayed
in my room 24/7 and tried to sleep while slouching in a cushioned
chair. Her sleeping arrangements were quite uncomfortable because
she couldn't lie down, but Mom wouldn't leave me.

Airlift

Every night that first week, we had a late visitor: Coach Schiano. He
would arrive by helicopter around eleven o'clock and maintain a vigil
for a couple of hours. Throughout the year, Coach had a helicopter
at his disposal so that he could save time traveling around New Jersey for recruiting and speaking engagements. It took him about nine
minutes to fly from Rutgers to Hackensack, a trip that could take up
to two hours if the New Jersey Turnpike was backed up.

I don't know how he had time to see me, because once our visit was over, he flew back to New Brunswick, drove home, grabbed a few hours of sleep, then got up and presided over early morning team meetings, which started at 7:15 A.M. Football practice then followed.

Coach Schiano treated me with warmth and love. I knew he really cared about my welfare and was grieved by what happened on the field. He truly was there for me when the chips were down. The first conversation I remember happened after my tracheotomy, when I mumbled this question: "How are you doing, Coach?"

His eyes glistened. He was thinking, *Are you kidding? You're asking me how I am doing?*

"I'm doing fine, Eric, but everyone in the Rutgers family is pulling for you," Coach replied. "The guys can't stop talking about you in the locker room. They are praying for your recovery."

Coach did most of the speaking because of the tubes in my mouth and the ventilator. He was never in a hurry to go and would hang out and chat with other family members and visitors after coming to my bedside. We grew very close from those late-night visits, and Coach Schiano became lot more than a coach to me.

In coming weeks, Coach realized that I wasn't leaving the hospital any day soon, so he set up a system where he would grab a graduate assistant—one of the player development guys—and have the GA drive him to Hackensack. It was usually a forty-five to sixty-minute ride to Hackensack, so Coach would get some work done before he arrived around 11 P.M. Then the graduate assistant would sleep in the car while Coach stayed at my bedside.

One time, I remember dozing off and waking up to the sight of him sitting in a chair with a computer on his lap, watching videos of our opponents' tendencies—work he would have done at a decent hour back in Piscataway. On another occasion, I woke up and saw that he had fallen asleep in his chair from exhaustion, computer still on his lap. Sometime in the early morning hours, he'd wake up from his nap and make the long trudge home.

How he did it with so little sleep during the middle of football season is something I'll never know and always appreciate.

Angels in My Presence

I liked having Coach Schiano and my immediate family with me in my ICU unit. Mom hit the wall, however, after an emotional first week. Sleeping in a cushioned armchair gave her no rest at all. Coach Schiano told her she had to get some decent sleep.

Mom knew good coaching when she heard it, so she let Rutgers reserve a hotel room around the corner from the medical center. Once I fell asleep for the night, she'd go to her hotel room. Sometimes she slept only five hours, but those solid-as-a-rock sleeping hours rejuvenated her.

While I was awake, though, I needed her by my side at all times.

"No, don't go!" I protested one night when she was about to head to the hotel to sleep. I wasn't tired, but she needed toothpicks to keep her eyes open. I wanted Mom to be there until my eyelids shut down for the night, because of my fear of the unknown.

Everything was new those first few weeks at Hackensack—my surroundings, my nurses and doctors, the smells and sounds, and the commotion. I hadn't come to grips with what happened on the 25-yard line during the Rutgers-Army game.

While I was in ICU, a nurse named Angelique sensed that Mom had nothing left to give and said she'd pinch-hit for Mom. "You get some rest," said Angelique. "I'll stay with Eric and won't leave him." The nurse rubbed my head until I fell asleep, and true to her word, she was still with me at 7:30 in the morning when Mom returned.

My sister Nicole and Auntie Cheryl took time off from work to be by my side. I liked having my older sister in the vicinity because she had a unique talent: she could read my lips better than anyone else. I'd try to speak a few words and Mom would say, "What's he saying? What's he saying?"

Nicole, from across the room, would say, "Oh, Mom. He's saying 'I'm hungry.' "

I was fed through a feeding tube because my doctors wanted to see how liquids were going down my throat. They wanted to be sure everything was going straight to my stomach and not into my lungs.

I wasn't ready for real food yet—that kind of swallow test would come several weeks later. But for now, my doctors were vitally interested in how my throat was working—and if the surgery to straighten my fractured vertebrae would be successful.

This was a big deal because my doctors were intimating to Mom that I might never be able to eat solid foods again.

Again, she didn't let me hear about those discussions because she wanted me to focus on getting better, figuring we could deal with the eating issue down the road. In the meantime, Mom knew that I'd be greatly interested in watching Rutgers's next football game, which was on the first Friday night of my hospital stay. The Scarlet Knights had won the first five out of seven games, and we were looking to keep it going against the University of Pittsburgh Panthers on the road.

I can't describe the bittersweet feelings swirling inside of me when Mom turned on the Rutgers-Pitt game at Hackensack and I saw my teammates running onto the field to start the game. There was a certainly a feeling of pride because my teammates were taking on another Big East opponent on a nationally televised game on ESPN. That delight, however, was tempered by a profound sadness because I couldn't be out there on the field, wearing my No. 52 jersey. I would have loved streaking down the field for the opening kickoff, straight-arming blockers and making open-field tackles.

It wasn't long before the cameras focused on a Rutgers player with a shiny BELIEVE sticker attached to the front of his helmets, a fact that caught the eyes of the ESPN Regional broadcasters, Mike Gleason and John Congemi.

The ESPN men in the booth described how the Rutgers community had rallied behind this message of support and how even Pittsburgh fans were behind me. As fans passed through the turnstiles for the Rutgers-Pittsburgh game, they were handed stickers saying "Pitt Is Pulling for Eric LeGrand." A banner with the same tribute was unfurled inside the stadium. My name was mentioned over the PA system, and fans heard a short update about my condition, which brought forth a moment of applause.

As the game progressed, however, I couldn't believe my eyes. It was like my teammates were playing on eggshells. They looked lackluster and lethargic on the field. I saw my roommate, Khaseem Greene, throw a shoulder into a running back instead of tackling him head-on and wrapping him up. It was like he was afraid to tackle properly, lest he end up in the hospital bed like I did. We lost, 41–21, to Pittsburgh, and it was clear that what had happened to me against Army a week earlier had taken an emotional toll on the team.

When Coach Schiano visited me on Sunday night, the day after the Pittsburgh game, I said to him, "Here is what you got to do, Coach. Tell them that my situation was a freak accident. They can't worry about it. They have to go out there and play as hard as they can."

Coach listened, and I could see the wheels turning. Coaching a team isn't as easy as it looks from an armchair or a hospital bed.

The trouble was that my teammates knew one of their own

was missing in action, and that uncertainty would play itself out
through the rest of the 2010 season.

No Negativity

Mom delivered a different type of pep talk to those wishing to see
me, and it was this: "Anybody who goes into that room to see Eric
cannot bring any negativity. It's got to be all positive."

Mom felt that any thoughts focusing on what I didn't have—
like the use of my arms and legs—would only reinforce the paralysis
seizing my body. Instead, visitors had to focus on the positive:

We can't wait to see you walk again.

You will use your arms again.

You won't have to be in a wheelchair the rest of your life.

Hearing all those nice things bolstered my confidence, and my
attitude mirrored what I was telling everyone who dropped by:

Yeah, I'm going to be fine.

I'll walk again. I'm sure of it.

This will just take a little time, that's all.

There isn't going to be a problem.

It was hard to stay awake and make small talk with everyone.
I tried to keep myself calm and all that, but there were hundreds of
people trying to see me. At least, that's what it seemed like the first
couple of weeks. When family, friends, and well-wishers came into
my ICU unit, though, they lifted my spirits because I received nothing but positive energy from them. I really thought I was going be
fine. *Maybe your body needs some downtime because of how hard
you've been going for the past three years at Rutgers,* I thought. *You
finally get to rest a little bit.*

In my mind, I thought I would be back on my feet sooner rather than later. Everything would be a lot better once I started a rehab program and began working to regain the use of my arms and legs.

Was I in denial? Was I unaware of the severity of my injuries?

Not really. In the beginning it was hard to wrap my brain around everything. But I honestly believed everything was going to be all right. A Bob Marley song, "Three Little Birds," kept swirling in my mind about everything being all right and not worrying about a thing.

The reggae-beat song became a mantra of sorts. Everything would be all right if I believed it would be. I asked Mom to play "Three Little Birds" over and over on a little iPod. The next time I saw Coach Schiano, I listened to the song with him and asked if he would play it for all the guys during practice.

"Sure, I'll do that," Coach Schiano said.

Coach followed through. A few days later, several guys from the team dropped by, and one asked me, "Hey, did you pick out that Bob Marley song?"

"Yeah, I did," I answered with a sheepish smile.

Knowing that my teammates were jamming to "Little Three Birds" during practice made me feel good. So did the time when I looked over and saw Mom and Nicole dancing to the reggae beat. They were doing what they could to get me feeling upbeat about my future.

Positive Energy Everywhere

Even though I had all this positive energy around me, I was still too tired many days to even sing along with my favorite songs coming out of the iPod.

I could barely keep my eyes open when I saw my first therapist. She was a short lady dressed in nurse's scrubs who came into my room and tried to move my legs. Then she touched my arms. She was moving me here and touching me there when I fell asleep on her. I was gone. I had no idea where I was.

Meanwhile, Mom was pouring all her energy into me—looking after my welfare, staying on top of the nurses, and lifting my spirits as high as she could. She brightened up the ICU with stuffed animals, football helmets, and posters of me playing football. Of course, Mom was human like the rest of us, and the combination of lack of sleep and the never-ending parade of visitors took its toll.

Unfortunately, she coped by smoking. Mom knew she shouldn't be lighting up. She had tried to quit before my injury, but she had started smoking again because it released the tension building up within her. She'd go outside and puff on a cigarette, which made her feel better. It didn't matter what the temperature was outside; she would have her smoke breaks during the day. Being outside was also a place where she could get away with her thoughts, even cry. And she cried because the sight of me lying on my back with a ventilator and a zillion machines and monitors connected to me overwhelmed her at times.

Of course, she never cried in front of me. She stayed strong. She had her good days and her bad days, which was certainly understandable since I had my ups and downs as well. We were in the midst of a waiting game to see how extensive the damage was and what my prognosis would be.

The main thing, Mom felt, was that I had to be in a good frame of mind and stay positive. That turned out to be a lot easier than any of us expected because of all the support I received. From the moment I spun and hit the turf in the New Meadowlands Stadium, I impacted people's lives all across the country and bonded with the New Jersey football community.

ESPN is responsible for the former, I would suppose. The producers of the various *SportsCenter* and *College GameDay* shows displayed great interest in keeping viewers up to date with my situation. There's no doubt that a college football player making a thunderous hit that left him immobile from the neck down was newsworthy and compelling. And there were visuals to go along with the story: all the producers had to do to underscore the seriousness of my plight was to replay the bone-crunching video of the kickoff—and viewers saw how I hit the ground and never got back up.

Thousands of people were moved by what they witnessed and went out of their way to write me letters of encouragement. Many were addressed, "Eric LeGrand, Rutgers Football Team, New Jersey," but they still found their way to my hospital bed. Nicole used to sit in my room and read them to me by the dozens.

Dear Eric,

My thoughts and prayers go out to you. God will see you through this, I know He will. Miracles are around us every day. We just have to look for them. Get well soon, No. 52.

Dear Eric,

You are not, nor will you ever be alone. Attack this injury with the same tenacity that you played the game. You and your family are in our prayers.

Other letters came through official channels from head coaches like Bill Belichick of the New England Patriots, Joe Paterno at Penn State, and Lane Kiffin with the University of Southern California Trojans. Hearing Nicole read their words of encouragement meant a great deal to me as well.

My jaw dropped when two NFL head coaches—Tom Coughlin of the New York Giants and Andy Reid of the Philadelphia Eagles—dropped by Hackensack to deliver their encouragement *in person*. I

had seen them on television many times before, but actually meeting
and talking with them was a thrill. Coach Coughlin brought a Giants helmet signed by the players and wanted me to know the entire
team was pulling for me. I was impressed by how Coach Coughlin
told reporters afterward what an incredible job Mom was doing
and how committed she was to keeping my spirits high.

Coach Reid stepped inside my hospital room during his bye
week. Philly is a good eighty-mile drive from Hackensack, so I was
impressed that he would travel all that distance to check in with me.
He would make two more personal visits, *and* he even got into the
habit of calling me on Sunday morning game days, which I have a
hard time believing today. What a great man.

The bulk of my emotional encouragement, though, came from
tens of thousands messages posted by strangers on websites like
nj.com, the portal for the *Star-Ledger* newspaper, or a Web page
that the Rutgers athletic department hurriedly set up.

It was hard not to get emotional when reading the messages:

*Eric, on behalf of our family and season ticket holders in
Section 110, we are praying for you. Please know you have
not only the entire Rutgers community behind you but millions of other Americans who have become aware of your
condition through the media. We will all be there for you,
regardless of your needs. As challenging and scary things
might be right now, please be reassured that you are getting
access to the best care in the world, and the community will
be there for you and your family. God bless you, and we
look forward to a full recovery!*

*Eric, you probably don't remember me, but we both played
baseball in Woodbridge Little League. You were actually
the first player to ever hit a home run off of me—and it*

didn't just scrape the top of the fence either! I'll never forget
that hit and how I thought to myself, "Damn, this kid is a
monster." I wish nothing but the best for you and for you
to heal as quickly as possible.

Many people wanted to offer a more tangible form of support, and to meet that demand, Rutgers helped Mom establish the "Eric LeGrand Believe Fund" as a collection point for the money donations coming in from many directions.

"The call to action is a practical answer to the emotional pain that has gripped us all in the wake of LeGrand's injury," wrote Tara Sullivan, a columnist for the *Record* in north New Jersey. "The depth of injury is so incalculable, so unimaginable, it is almost too difficult to contemplate. Yet people not directly connected to the LeGrand family or the Rutgers program still find themselves overwhelmed by the sense of what the family is going through. That is where the need for a practical outlet comes in," she wrote.

The idea was to establish a fund that would help us out with expenses or long-term care not covered by my health insurance. Even though we had three "lines of defense"—Mom's health insurance through her work, the Rutgers's football team insurance company, and the NCAA insurance plan—these three insurance plans didn't cover everything.

In addition, there were the day-to-day costs of living that were not covered by insurance: Mom's mortgage on the home in Avenel, gas and upkeep for the car, utilities, food, incidentals, etc. Mom could no longer work, because she had a round-the-clock job as my caregiver. After exhausting her sick and vacation pay six weeks after my injury, she had to quit her job as an import/export specialist.

It's been said that a spinal cord injury is a financially crippling injury. Mom can only shake her head at what would have happened to us if we only had her health insurance from work. If that were the case, we would have been on the hook for 20 to 30 percent of the costs. Thank God we had the Rutgers and NCAA insurance to cover that gap as well as other major expenses. I heard Mom say that the only fortunate aspect of my spinal cord injury is that it occurred while I was playing college football in an NCAA-sanctioned event. Otherwise, we would be financially bankrupt and receive a far lower standard of health care.

The cost of a catastrophic spinal cord injury would blow your mind. The first two days at Hackensack alone cost a quarter of a million dollars. That was just the tip of the iceberg: I was in the Hackensack ICU for three weeks, stayed at the Kessler Institute for Rehabilitation for five months, and ever since then I have required daily nursing care every day and will for the rest of my life unless I make dramatic improvements.

Then there have been significant purchases like a $40,000 wheelchair, nearly $10,000 for a Hoyer Lift and a microAIR Mattress, thousands more for special exercise equipment with electrodes to stimulate my muscles and a mat table—the list is quite extensive. When you add up everything that's been spent so far—hospitalization, rehabilitation, and ongoing nursing care, Mom says we're nearing the $1 million mark.

That's why the establishment of the Eric LeGrand Believe Fund as well as the Eric LeGrand Patriot Saint Foundation within a week of my injury left me feeling humbled. The Eric LeGrand Patriot Saint Foundation was established by my old Pop Warner coach, Jack Nevins, who's president of an executive board comprised of parents from Woodbridge Township who grew up with me and stood in grandstands with Mom watching me run for touchdowns, hit home runs, or sink three-point shots on the basketball court.

News that old-time friends of the family as well as perfect strangers were digging deep into their pockets to help Mom and me lifted my spirits to incredible heights. But what I appreciated just as much, if not more, were nonmonetary displays of support. Within a few days of my injury, Scott Kaye and Mike Frauenheim, both sales representatives for the Riddell sporting apparel company, came up with a plan to donate sixteen thousand No. 52 helmet decals to as many New Jersey high school football teams as they could. Just mapping out the driving routes to get all the stickers to the teams was quite a logistical effort.

Steve Ostergren of Scarlet Fever, a Rutgers fan shop in New Brunswick, had scarlet T-shirts with ERIC BELIEVE NO. 52 printed on the front and KEEP CHOPPING on the back. Students lined up around the corner to purchase more than one hundred thousand dollars' worth of T-shirts in the first month. Students at Caldwell College in Caldwell, New Jersey, sold thousands of wristbands with my name to raise funds. And in months to come, a variety of fund-raisers would be held on my behalf: a conglomerate of New Brunswick restaurants selling tickets for a set menu and donating at least half the proceeds for the "We Believe Dines Out" program; 5K walks and motorcycle runs; charity bowling events with NFL celebrities; former Giants receiver David Tyree competing in a tough-man challenge with me as the beneficiary; bake sales at Colonia Middle School; and a variety of wristbands and T-shirts, many with BELIEVE imprinted on the band or silkscreened on the shirt.

A billboard company donated a digital billboard on the New Jersey Turnpike that had a head shot of me, the word BELIEVE, and the address of the Eric LeGrand Believe Fund. Nicole nearly choked on the apple she was eating the first time she saw the billboard while driving to visit me at Hackensack.

The "Believe" story took a life of its own and became the motto for the Rutgers football team after my injury. Beginning with the Pittsburgh game, the offense broke every huddle with a handclap and chanting "Believe!" in unison.

The Other Leg of Support

On October 29, 2010, just thirteen days after my injury, the Rutgers team chaplain, John Maurer, organized a rally at the College Avenue gymnasium. Attendance was voluntary, but most of the Rutgers football team was there as well as students and friends.

One of our defensive team captains, Joe Lefeged, got up to say a few words. "Eric is probably the strongest guy on our football team inside and out, and God would not put this in front of him if he could not move through this," he said.

My aunt Cheryl told the audience, "Although Eric suffered a serious injury, his mind and his spirit are intact. He told a physical therapist, 'Don't challenge me—you will lose.' He's stubborn, he's a fighter. We have no doubt he'll come through this."

Coach Schiano was the last to speak, and he told those attending the rally that it had been a very tough time for the Rutgers family. "But to the people sitting here tonight, I don't know a whole lot about medicine, and some would say I don't know a whole lot about anything lately," Coach said. "But you know that God answers our prayers, and I believe the number-one thing we can do is encourage people to pray for Eric. He knows what has to be done, and his set of challenges have changed. But you know what? Eric is a guy who never backs down from a challenge. He will walk again. I believe that."

Coach then asked everyone at the rally to stand up and join in a clapping exercise that he led the team in at the start of every morning practice.

This is how *Star-Ledger* columnist Steve Politi described what happened next:

> "Come on," the football coach turned preacher said. "Get up now. If you truly believe that this is going to be done through God, then let's hear it for God and what He's going to do."
>
> He started slapping his hands together, his navy blazer flapping as his arms moved.
>
> *Clap clap clap clap clap clap clap.*
>
> "No, no, no!" he yelled as the fans turned parishioners tried to stop. "God can't hear that, guys!"
>
> He started moving, from one side of the stage to the other, his race reddening from the exertion.
>
> "Let's go!"
>
> *CLAP CLAP CLAP CLAP CLAP CLAP CLAP CLAP CLAP CLAP CLAP!*
>
> The applause turned into a cheer, and suddenly, the room felt like an opening kickoff was seconds away.

"Opening kickoff" was an interesting choice of words given how I became injured, but Coach Schiano, Aunt Cheryl, Uncle Ariel, and team chaplain John Maurer would become my spiritual rocks of support after my injury. My aunt and uncle were strong Christians who took their faith seriously and were heavily involved with their church, The Cathedral, a Bible-teaching church located in Perth Amboy near the New Jersey coast. I had gone occasionally to their church growing up, but I wouldn't say that Mom and I were consistent churchgoers in my younger years.

As for Coach Schiano, he had always worn his Christian faith on his coaching sleeve. He liked to joke that without his faith he never would have gotten through his first few years at Rutgers, when the team was losing so many games, but he saw coaching as a way to impact players' lives—almost as a ministry.

Coach had become a Christian while he was a defensive assistant coach with the Chicago Bears in the mid-1990s. The way the story goes, the Bears' director of college scouting at the time, Mike McCartney, gave Coach Schiano a cassette tape of his father, Bill McCartney—a football coach at the University of Colorado and founder of the Christian men's organization Promise Keepers—speaking at a prayer breakfast.

During his drive home from work, Coach listened to Bill McCartney talk about the negative effect football had on his family life in a message that included a call to believe in Jesus Christ and give his life to him. Affected in a mighty way, Coach pulled over to the side of the road and repeated the prayer at the end of the tape. His life changed that day.

As for John Maurer, I had met the Rutgers team chaplain during my freshman year. He was part of Athletes in Action, a sports ministry working with college and professional athletes. At the beginning of the season, John invited the players to participate in a small group Bible study or meet with him individually.

That sounded like a good idea to me because I was new on campus and feeling my way around. I wasn't sure who I was yet, and I was open to hearing about what really matters in life. You could say that I was trying to figure things out after I left home, enrolled in college, and was on my own.

I participated in one of John's introductory Bible studies to the Christian life with three or four other players my freshman year, and I enjoyed myself. I learned the building blocks of Christianity: that the Bible teaches us that everyone has sinned, that the penalty

for sin is death, that Jesus Christ died for our sins, and to be for-
given of our sins, salvation is a free gift to those who believe in Jesus
Christ.

John planted some important seeds, but like the Parable of the
Sower, some of those seeds took root and grew, while the pressures
of the world choked some of the seeds. I drifted away from the Bible
study my sophomore year. I can't point to any specific reason why
except that life was incredibly busy with football and schoolwork.
John and I continued to be friendly, however, and I always enjoyed
our conversations. He was a good listener.

And then the major crisis happened in my life on that October
day, and these four special people were there for me in my hour of
need. We shared powerful times of prayer during some of my lowest
moments when I was confronted with a pessimistic prognosis that I
may never walk again. I'll never forget the times when Aunt Cheryl,
Uncle Ariel, and Coach Schiano would gather around my hospital
bed and pray out loud to God to work a special miracle in my life
and heal me.

A few days after my surgery, Aunt Cheryl asked if she could
read Psalm 23 to me. I could barely move my head, so I was nearly
immobilized. I needed hope during a time of despair.

She opened her Bible and read these centuries-old words that
soothed my troubled soul:

The Lord is my shepherd, I lack nothing.
He makes me lie down in green pastures, he leads me
    beside quiet waters, he refreshes my soul. He guides me
    along the right paths for his name's sake.
Even though I walk through the darkest valley, I will fear
    no evil, for you are with me; your rod and your staff,
    they comfort me.
You prepare a table before me in the presence of my

enemies. You anoint my head with oil; my cup
overflows.
Surely your goodness and love will follow me all the days
of my life, and I will dwell in the house of the Lord
forever.

Those sentences lifted my spirits, especially the part walking
through the darkest valley. That's where I was—the darkest valley. It didn't get any darker, if you asked me. But the psalmist reminded me that the Lord was with me and His rod and His staff
comforted me.

I couldn't help but be struck by the irony of the use of the word
walking through the darkest valley. There I was, lying in a hospital
bed in an ICU unit, hooked up to every kind of machine there was,
and I couldn't walk at all. I wasn't regaining any feelings or the ability to move any muscles below my neck.

When you lay in a hospital bed every waking moment, you have
a lot of time to think.

A lot of deep thoughts were going through my mind, like:

Why did this injury happen to me?

Why did God allow this to happen to me?

What had I done wrong?

I had some awesome conversations with John Maurer discussing
heavy questions on my mind. I was not angry with God. Confused,
yes. But not angry. My mind constantly played with the what-ifs:

- What if the kickoff had veered off the right instead of
  to the left?
- What if those blockers had succeeded in bottling me up
  and keeping me away from the return man?
- What if I hit Malcolm Brown a little differently and not
  with the tip of my helmet?

John told me that the Lord had not forsaken me, that He knew exactly where I was and what I was dealing with, and God never does anything by accident, even in a tragedy like I had experienced. God's thoughts were not our thoughts, John said. He had a plan for my life, and unfortunately, this pain and suffering was part of it. Our discussions helped me come to a place where all I could do was trust in God . . . trust Him for the outcome.

Aunt Cheryl noted many of the same things. "Eric, everything that's happened is not for nothing," she said. "I don't think this is just for you, this accident on the football field. I believe you have the opportunity to speak to people, to bless them with your words, and bring attention to this type of spinal cord injury. I believe God has a purpose and a plan for you, just as He says in His Word." And then Auntie Cheryl read Jeremiah 29:11 from the Old Testament, which profoundly touched me:

> *"For I know the plans I have for you," declares the Lord,*
> *"plans to prosper you and not to harm you, plans to*
> *give you hope and a future."*

Plans to give me hope and a future.

As crazy as it sounds, what Aunt Cheryl said made sense. What happened at New Meadowlands Stadium that day was part of God's plan for me. I didn't know why that was His plan for me, but it was. Coming to this realization helped me put some of the pieces together. Not the entire puzzle, but enough pieces to see a picture emerging.

God still cared about me, still had a plan for my life. He had not abandoned me on that football field. I decided that the greatest thing I had going was to trust in God's plan, whatever it was.

Trusting in God helped me have a great attitude. If I could remain upbeat and positive in the face of such a devastating turn of events, then I would be doing everything God was asking of me.

My childlike faith grew in those days. I didn't know where I was heading, but I had hope for the future—hope beyond my days here on earth, hope that my future was more than life in a wheelchair and then it was all over.

I heard it said that we can live thirty days without food, three days without water, three minutes without air but only seconds without hope.

I needed hope most of all.

11

MAKING THE MOVE TO KESSLER

After three weeks or so at Hackensack, the doctors began discussing my future. No one on my medical team had yet told me just how challenging the road ahead might be or that there was a huge possibility I might never walk again. What they were telling me was that my life would soon be consumed by rehabilitation sessions.

I couldn't imagine what "rehab" meant for someone who couldn't move his arms or legs, but I knew I would be starting from scratch, coaxing my muscles to get moving again. Nothing was going to happen overnight. I would be rebuilding brick by brick.

Mom huddled up with Nicole and Aunt Cheryl to discuss my options. They were told to check out the Kessler Institute for Rehabilitation in West Orange, New Jersey. When I heard that they were taking a road trip to visit Kessler, I wanted at least one of them to stay behind because this would be the first time I would be all by myself. But Mom told me that it was really important for the three of them to tour the Kessler Institute facility together.

For more than sixty years, the Kessler Institute had pioneered the course of physical medicine and rehabilitation. Kessler set the gold standard when it came to providing highly specialized care, advanced treatment, and leading-edge technologies for those with spinal cord injuries. Kessler also rehabilitated stroke victims, those who'd lost a limb, and individuals with all sorts of neurological disorders.

During their tour, Mom, Nicole, and Aunt Cheryl learned that Kessler was where actor Christopher Reeve spent the first six months of recovery after an excruciating fall left him a quadriplegic.

I hadn't watched any *Superman* movies growing up, but Mom and my family members had, and they told me Christopher Reeve was quite the Superman onscreen and off. Talented and good-looking, he was a superb athlete who did his own stunts. He was an expert sailor, scuba diver, and skier. By the 1990s, he had found a new passion: riding horses. He loved to compete in show-jumping events.

In May 1995, Christopher was riding his Thoroughbred, Eastern Express, through a course when his horse suddenly balked at a rail jump, pitching him forward. His hands got tangled in the horse's bridle, and he landed headfirst, fracturing the uppermost vertebrae in his spine and instantly paralyzing him from the neck down.

Like me, Christopher was unable to breathe, and only prompt medical attention saved his life. He suffered the worse fracture possible on his spinal column when he shattered his C1 and C2 vertebrae. Doctors had to literally reattach his head to his spine. When Christopher came out of surgery and was told about what happened along with a dire prognosis, he wondered to his wife, Dana, if "maybe we should let me go."

"But you're still you, and I love you," she said—words that gave him a will to live.

During my family's tour of Kessler, they were impressed with a large, airy, gymlike wing where spinal cord injury victims went through their rehabilitation exercises. Much of the funding for this facility came from the Christopher and Dana Reeve Foundation because this was the place where Reeve received rehabilitation when he was alive. Kessler was one of only seven centers in the United States with a rehabilitation program like this for spinal cord injury victims.

The rehabilitation program was open to individuals with complete or incomplete spinal cord injuries—those who were either totally paralyzed with no sensation below the level of injury or those who had some voluntary contraction or movement in their limbs. The primary focus of this intensive activity-based intervention was to promote recovery by retraining the nervous system.

My family witnessed several spinal cord injury victims having their muscles worked on by physical therapists or by special, high-tech-looking machines that moved the extremities for the patient. Everywhere my family looked, there was a sense of peace within this nurturing environment. Mom was particularly impressed.

They returned to Hackensack with a glowing report. "Eric, you're going to love it," Mom said. "They've got all the latest equipment, and everything was state of the art."

I listened, intrigued, but then Mom dropped a bombshell on me.

"Kessler can take you in a few days," she said.

"A few days? Why so soon?" It seemed like we were rushing into this. I had been in the Hackensack hospital for only three weeks. I had lost all my strength and didn't feel like I was in any shape to be moved yet.

"Eric, you've got to start rehab. That's the only way you'll get better," Mom said.

"But I don't know if I'm ready," I replied. I mean, I wanted to get better, but as an athlete, I knew I needed to regroup before I took things to the next level. Perhaps there was a part of me that feared that if I started rehabilitation and didn't see immediate improvement, I'd lose hope.

"But, Sweetie, the faster you start rehab, the faster you can regain the use of your arms and legs."

I didn't know what to say. I knew deep down that my body wasn't ready. I needed more rest. This wasn't the right time.

Nobody was hearing me, or even if they were, they thought they knew better. Both my sister and aunt chimed in about how great Kessler was going to be.

I figured they knew more than I did, so I gave in, but deep inside, I didn't have a sense of peace. We were rushing into this before my body was ready. Despite my misgivings, Mom thought we should move ahead, so that's what we did.

On Wednesday, November 3, the day I was transferred, Mom issued a statement through Rutgers University: "Eric is in good spirits and is anxious to take the next step in his rehabilitation process. Thank you to everyone for the tremendous outpouring of love, support, and prayers for Eric." She also requested privacy as we transitioned to this next phase of care and treatment.

I was once again carefully moved from my bed to a wheeled stretcher and transported in an EMT vehicle to West Orange, around eighteen miles or forty-five minutes away. Kessler had inpatient care and outpatient services; I needed the 'round-the-clock inpatient care, of course.

On the way to Kessler, something inside my stomach went crazy, and I felt nauseated. I certainly wasn't myself. If I was hoping for a quiet time of transition, it didn't happen. No sooner had I been taken to my room when a steady stream of visitors arrived to welcome me to Kessler. There were family and friends, therapists, aides, nurses, my case manager, and even Kessler's CEO in West Orange, Bonnie Evans, who assured me that I was in the best place possible. "If there is anything you need, you be sure to let us know, because we care here at Kessler," she said.

Even though it was nice that everyone made such an effort, I wasn't feeling up for the welcome wagon. The hoopla overwhelmed me. Then I was introduced to my new nurse's aide, a Jamaican-looking dude named Humphrey who looked about five feet, four inches and 110 pounds soaking wet.

"Yeah, mon, I'm gonna be the guy taking care of you. I'm gonna be lifting you and getting you dressed," he said in a lilting Caribbean accent.

"You're gonna lift me up and get me ready?" I wasn't sure if I heard right. He was the same size as I was back in fourth grade.

"Yeah, mon. Donna worry. You'll see."

I didn't see how it was possible that he could lift me from the bed and into a wheelchair. I hated being a burden to others. A feeling of helplessness washed over me, not being able to do anything for myself. My greatest wish was to get out of my bed under my own power, but no matter how much I desired that to happen, my body could not respond.

A profound feeling of sadness threatened to drown me, and when everyone finally cleared out of my room, I lay in my bed, alone with my thoughts.

Rutgers Travels to Florida

My mood improved when the Rutgers football game came on at eight o'clock that evening. My teammates would be playing the University of South Florida on ESPN. This would be one of those unusual Wednesday night games.

Rheanne came over from New Brunswick to watch the game with me, and Mom and Nicole were there, too. I have to say that it was nice to forget about my troubles for a few hours because Rutgers's road game against South Florida turned out to be one those entertaining "track meets"—a game where both offenses moved the ball at will. As the game wore on, though, I became more agitated and had no patience for anything, including the TV timeouts.

Rheanne noticed there was something off about me. "Eric, what's wrong with you?" she said. "You need to relax."

How could I chill? Didn't she know there was a strong possibility I'd never walk again? This was a thought that rarely crossed my mind—and something I didn't believe. But I also was not in denial. When this fleeting thought came to mind, I would focus on the positive. Focus on my faith and my plans—God's plans for my life. But on this particular night, I couldn't seem to shake my attitude. I didn't feel like myself.

We took a 24–17 lead into the third quarter but then things got out of hand. A South Florida field goal cut into our lead, 24–20, then Chas Dodd gambled with a screen pass on our 3-yard line that ended with a safety. We were still ahead 24–22 and had a big interception on South Florida's 36-yard line, but all we got out of it was a field goal.

Now we were up 27–22 and needed the defense to make a fourth-quarter stop. We didn't. We let South Florida score in five plays to grab the lead, 28–27 (their two-point conversation failed)—and here's where my memory ends. Whether it was the lateness of the hour—it was nearing midnight—or my frustration with how the game was playing out, I fell asleep.

In a deep, deep sleep.

Rheanne and Nicole were fighting yawns, so they left. Rheanne returned to Rutgers, and Nicole departed for home. Mom, of course, stayed; she would sleep on an uncomfortable chair that pulled out into a short bed.

Right before the South Florida game finished (a game we would lose), I woke up and started acting weird. My eyes were so scary-looking that Mom shook me and slapped me lightly in the face. But I didn't respond. She felt as though I was looking right through her.

"Eric, snap out of it!" she said.

"Hit me again," I said in my delirium. My body also felt like it was on fire, and in my feverishness, I had no idea Mom was yelling at me to get a grip. "Eric, calm down!" said the voice I didn't recognize.

The next thing I knew, I was on a stretcher and being wheeled down a long hallway. I tried to train my eyes on what was happening around me, but it felt like I was looking at the world through fogged-out goggles. And my body was so warm.

Mom was walking besides me. I asked her a question. "Am I cross-eyed, Mom?"

"No, but you need to close your eyes," she replied. My eyes *were* cross-eyed, so much so that she thought my eyes would pop out of my skull at any moment.

I kept trying to move my arms. Why didn't they move? And my hands? Why couldn't I twiddle my fingers?

More efforts to move my arms drew upon all the strength and exertion I once had, but nothing would happen. And then I blacked out. Mercifully.

The next thing I knew, I woke up in an emergency room. I was behind a partitioned curtain with my mother and sister. I recognized both of them. (Mom had called Nicole, who turned around immediately.)

"Hey, Nicole, are we going to IHOP today?" I always liked going to the International House of Pancakes growing up. They had great pancakes and waffles.

"What's wrong with you?" Nicole demanded.

"I want to go to IHOP. I feel like pancakes."

"Eric, go back to sleep."

"No." I tried to get up, but I couldn't. Nicole had to be sitting on me, just like she did when I was a kindergartner. "Get off me right now," I said.

"Eric, I'm not on you."

"Get off of me! I want to get out of here!"

I put my head down and allowed myself to fall into a daze. Meanwhile, Mom called Dr. Robert Monaco, the Rutgers team doctor, to tell him about the emergency. Dr. Monaco was in the South Florida visitors locker room with the team, and when he heard Mom say that I was delirious and might not make it, the team scrambled to the airport for the flight back to Newark. Coach Schiano feared that when the team plane touched down at Liberty International he'd hear I didn't make it.

I knew nothing about this, of course. After accusing Nicole of sitting on top of me, she tried to set me straight. "Eric, we're in the emergency room of Saint Barnabas Medical Center in Livingston. You had a little episode, so they're going to get us a room shortly."

A high fever had made me irrational. My body temperature had spiked to 105.5 degrees—a half of a degree from frying my brain. I was told later that high fevers were common for someone in my condition, and that I could also expect to be hit with pneumonia, urinary tract infections, and deep-vein thrombosis after suffering a severe spinal cord injury.

News that I had been rushed to Saint Barnabas was treated as a setback by the media. It was a scary situation for twelve hours, but I eventually came around.

Everything will be okay, I told myself. Just as I tell myself today my accident had a higher purpose, I now believe that incident happened for a reason. Several days at Saint Barnabas helped me find new perspective.

In the room next door to me at Saint Barnabas, a constant trail of visitors waited for their chance to say good-bye to a young woman in her early twenties. My nurses told me that she had suffered a brain aneurysm and wasn't expected to live much longer. I heard the muffled cries of grief and saw family members and friends wiping away tears in the hallway. Hearing those moans and sounds of crying caused me to become very upset. I was deeply moved because she was too young to die.

For this young woman I didn't even know, this was it. Her life would soon be over.

Meanwhile, I was alive. I didn't die on the football field. I had survived. So why had I lived and this young woman was about to die?

I didn't have any answers, but I recognized that even though I lay on a hospital bed, unable to move anything below my neck, I was still blessed. I still had things to be thankful for, and number one on the list was being alive. I had a family who loved me *and* wanted me to live. I had a Creator who knew exactly what I was going through.

The young woman next door died the following day, and I was profoundly sad even though we never met. *That could have been me.*

Five days later, I was transferred back to Kessler with a new-found outlook. I also got into a better frame of mind—a frame of mind that I had to have the same mental toughness I showed on the football field.

Mental toughness.

That was probably the strongest attribute I developed while playing football, and I knew I'd have to draw on my mental strength like never before.

Learning Curve

One of the mental challenges of becoming paralyzed was getting my head around the idea that I would not be able to take care of myself.

That was really hard—and is still the most difficult aspect of my life today. Take a simple thing like an itching nose. Before the injury, I'd rub my nose with one of my fingers and that would take care of the itch. Now I had to scrunch up my nose, wiggle my mouth, and stretch my facial muscles to satisfy the itch, but usually those actions didn't cut it. That's when I would ask Mom to draw closer so that I could rub my face against her arm or shoulder.

But if nobody was close enough to scratch my nose, a simple thing like a facial itch could be agony.

Everything was a learning curve, including getting used to my new motorized wheelchair. There was the time when Rheanne was hanging out in my room and went to put her right foot on one of the rubber tires. Instead her foot landed on the tilt button—which automatically tilted the back of my wheelchair.

The next thing I knew, I was suddenly thrust all the way back—an action that startled the both of us and nearly caused me to fall backward to the linoleum floor. As Rheanne got tangled up with the wheelchair and tried to stop me from spilling out, she got a pretty good bruise on her leg. After she got me straightened up, we ended up laughing about the mishap.

Another time, I was in my chair and Rheanne wanted to know if I could feel anything with my hands and fingers. She grabbed my right hand and brought my arm up toward her head. Mom had put some lotion on my hand an hour earlier, and my hand slipped Rheanne's grip and whacked my head.

I still tease Rheanne about the time she nearly gave me a black eye! Everyone chuckled when I half knocked myself silly, and being able to laugh about a trivial thing like that also took the edge off the tension in the room.

Anyone with a spinal cord injury still has feelings on and around his head, which is why I liked having people touch my head and my neck. I grew to especially enjoy those sensations whenever my dreadlocks were retwisted every three weeks.

I'm proud of my dreads and have been since I started wearing them as a senior at Colonia High. I got the idea for the dreadlock look when a hip-hop artist named E-40 rapped about dreads in his song "Tell Me When to Go." I continue to wear my dreads today, nearly two years after my injury. They seem to be my trademark because everyone knows me for them and, of course, for my smile. I think sometimes it amazes people that I still can muster such a big grin considering my circumstances.

It may seem like I didn't have much to smile about, but I never saw it that way. I was alive. I had a wonderful family who filled my room every day. I had friends and people I had never met rooting me on, and I knew that I would walk again. My comeback just would take time and patience. It was about this time that I started a practice of praying every night before I fell asleep, thanking God for everything I have.

As I discovered from other patients, life could be much worse. I had much to be thankful for, including how insurance covered a top-of-the-line Permobil C500. This high-tech motorized wheelchair came with a molded plastic mouthpiece that I could use to move around as I desired. Pressing the mouthpiece upward with my lips moved the wheelchair forward, while a nudge on either side would turn the wheelchair in any direction I wanted. Pressing *down* on the mouthpiece with my lips or chin stopped the wheelchair. You can only imagine how sensitive the mouthpiece is to the direction of my lips.

It took some practice getting used to moving around, but I had plenty of time to get the hang of it. The wheelchair represented a chance to get out of my hospital bed and roam the halls a little bit— and see new friends I was making at Kessler. Mom didn't have to wheel me to someone's room and then come back to get me.

It was a wonderful feeling to get some measure of independence back. Yes, I was still confined to a wheelchair and unable to move from the neck down, but I could move around on my own. The worst part about my accident was feeling like I was a burden to my family. A couple of months earlier, I had been a capable and strapping football player—the one always doing the heavy lifting. Now I was relying on others. The outpouring of help and support was beyond generous, but regaining some mobility with the wheelchair—well, that helped me feel more like the man I once was.

It was an adjustment going to therapy every day, however, because I didn't have much energy. I had two hours in the morning and an hour in the afternoon, and for the first month or two at Kessler, that's all I could handle.

But I was eager to do rehab. My therapists told me that their goal was to help me regain as much function as possible. To accomplish that, they would use methods to help my spinal column "remap" connections to paralyzed limbs, which meant physically retraining the legs and the trunk while reawakening the nervous system. I set the bar higher: I wanted to walk again, but I understood that to get there I first needed to regain motor function and sensation.

I had a responsibility to give rehab my best effort, just as I did on the football field. How could I let down the thousands of people behind me—those praying for me, those encouraging me, and those financially supporting the Believe Fund?

I couldn't, not after I heard about the raffle of a plush brown bear wearing my No. 52 Rutgers jersey that netted $600 in Perth Amboy. Not after the pinball tournament in Asbury Park that raised $1,000 on my behalf. Not after Erica Bowden, a Rutgers student, created red wristbands with the message "Eric LeGrand #52 Believe" written on them, bringing in $65,000. Not after Devin Harris, an NBA star with the New Jersey Nets, convinced Nets players, coaches, and ownership to donate $75,000 through Harris's "34 Ways to Assist Foundation."

Absolutely incredible. And there were so many other fund-raising efforts that I can't mention them all.

These are some of the reasons why I attacked my therapy at Kessler with the same intensity as when I started lifting weights in my basement back in eighth grade. That was my mentality—to embrace rehab and power through.

Regaining Weight

Shortly after arriving at Kessler, my throat and neck had healed enough for me to resume eating solid foods again. I didn't know it at the time, but I laid to rest any concerns my doctors had about whether I would have to be fed by a feeding tube the rest of my days.

For one of the few times in my life, I had some weight to regain because I had shed a great deal while being fed with a feeding tube. At one point during my rehabilitation, my weight dwindled to 196 pounds—a little bit lower than my playing weight as a high school freshman.

Now that the feeding tube had been removed, I started slowly by consuming soft, bland foods—oatmeal, mashed potatoes, apple-sauce, and sandwiches on soft bread. My appetite was awful, how-ever. It was like the desire to eat got shut off after being on a feeding tube for a couple of months.

Mom was concerned that I didn't want to eat, so she decided to do something about it. Each morning, she would leave the Kessler campus and drive to nearby West Orange. Her first stop was Dunkin' Donuts, where she'd buy me two vanilla-glazed doughnuts. Then she'd pass by McDonald's drive-thru and pick me up biscuits, hash browns, and an orange juice. These were some of my favorite comfort foods.

Mom would feed me breakfast as the nurses got me dressed for morning therapy. Toward noontime, Mom would slip out and return to the nearby McDonald's, where she knew my order by heart: cheeseburger (no lettuce, tomato, or pickle), large fries, Coke, and a chocolate milk shake.

If it was her goal to fatten me up, she succeeded. I did gain weight, and my appetite came back with a vengeance—so much so that we now have to watch that I don't gain *too* much weight, lest I get too big for my wheelchair.

Line out the Door

The support around me was amazing—the best anyone could hope for. It didn't take me long to realize that there were a lot of people at Kessler worse off than me. I was in the best possible situation for someone with a serious spinal cord injury.

The patients at Kessler were either very old or very young like myself—the victims of a horrible accident like a car crash or a diving mishap. Many of the patients received a handful of visitors each week, while I had a line out of the door every day with people wanting to see me. Sometimes my room at Kessler was so crowded with friends, teammates, and coaches that Coach Schiano could barely squeeze in. Coach was still making weekly trips to Kessler. He told the press that everyone needed to keep me in their prayers and not to forget me.

It was really nice not to be cast aside, but I was all too cognizant of other patients at Kessler who had been dismissed by family or didn't have any friends to visit them. I made it a point to engage these patients and let it be known I wanted them to come by my room, even if there were plenty of folks already there. In my mind, they could make friends with my friends. I realized that part of my new purpose in life was to reach out to those around me, especially those who did not have the support I had.

One of my therapists, Barbara, wanted me to meet a guy named Jermaine, who had cancer of the spine. Jermaine was a cool kid, just twenty-two years old. I didn't see his family around all that much, and he didn't seem to have the emotional support I did. I told him that he could chill in my room any time he wanted.

We got into a routine where he would play one of my all-time favorite video games, *Call of Duty,* on my TV. He still had use of his upper body, so I'd yell at him to do this or do that with the characters. We shared some great moments, and we helped each other pass the time.

Then his cancer started spreading to his head, causing him to become incoherent. He didn't know where he was or who people were. That was so sad. The only thing the doctors could do was give him painkilling medicines. I felt badly for him. I saw his family coming around more toward the end, but his situation reminded me that I couldn't take any of the encouragement I received for granted. When I left Kessler in the spring of 2011, Jermaine was still alive and undergoing radiation therapy for his cancer. Sadly, he passed away in June 2011.

It was interactions with terminally ill people like Jermaine that helped me get in the right frame of mind about my future. Not a day passed that I didn't feel blessed to still be alive and still have the power to remain positive.

My doctors, however, were telling Mom a different story. They told her there was a good chance I would never breathe on my own and that my spinal cord injury was "complete," which meant that there was a total lack of movement or sensation below the site of the injury. An "incomplete" designation would bring a more optimistic long-term outlook for recovery since that would mean key muscles below the level of injury were functional. Doctors told Mom that I wouldn't be able to move anything, including any of my shoulder muscles.

But Mom never discussed those conversations with me. She knew me best and didn't want me to get down on myself. She protected me from those who didn't understand how my belief in a happier outcome was strong enough to beat the odds.

All I knew was that I had a job to do, and that was to get myself healthy. The first order of business was to get off the ventilator, which made me very uncomfortable. It was one thing to lie in a bed and not be able to move, but dealing with a ventilator drove up my misery index. I didn't like the way the ventilator made it harder to talk. I didn't like the noise it made at night, which kept me awake. And I was still nervous that my vent would pop off and I wouldn't be able to breathe.

I hated the ventilator so much that one time I told my pulmonary nurse that I didn't need it anymore, a month after my injury. She spoke with my pulmonary doctor, Dr. Douglas Green, but they were both hesitant to take me off the ventilator because they didn't think my lungs were strong enough to carry the load. I felt going off the vent *would* make my lungs stronger, so I made my case to them. I believe I changed their minds because they saw the look of determination in my face.

"We can take you off the vent and see how you'll do," the nurse, after consulting the doctor, said, "but you'll be lucky to last a minute."

I took that as a challenge. The first time they shut down the ventilator, I went for an hour and a half breathing on my own. The next time, I went two hours . . . then a half day. I was breathing fine. When I get something into my head, I'll do whatever it takes to follow through, and in this situation, I was going to will myself off the vent.

Dr. Green and my pulmonary nurse were shocked that I could

breathe on my own so easily. They had not imagined such an outcome was possible. So it's understandable that they were reluctant to pack up the ventilator machine entirely, and they insisted that I stay on it during the night. Within a week or so, though, I convinced them that I didn't need the ventilator during the night, either. A few days before Thanksgiving, I was taken off the ventilator for good. Score one for the home team.

Encouraging News, Encouraging Visit

I scored another touchdown the same week when my doctors reclassified me from a complete spinal cord injury to an incomplete spinal cord injury.

A week or so after I was injured on the field, I was rolled onto my stomach and a needle—like a safety pin—was inserted into my anus.

If the anus closes—in other words, if the anal sphincter feels the needle (ouch!), you're considered to have an "incomplete" spinal cord injury. If there's no reaction to the needle prick, then you're considered to have a "complete" spinal cord injury.

In my situation, there was no reaction when the needle was inserted into my anus, so I was given an A Complete on the American Spinal Injury Association (ASIA) impairment scale, which ranges from A to E (A being a devastating complete injury and E being completely normal function).

When the same needle test was administered to me at Kessler, my anus *did* have a reaction. I actually felt the needle prick, and it kind of hurt, which means a message got through to the brain and told the anus to contract.

Because I now showed some sensory function, I was reclassified as a B Incomplete on the ASIA impairment scale. According to the chart, sensory but not motor function was preserved below the level of injury.

This was great news in our camp and a sign—albeit a small one—that my body was making some sort of neurological comeback. Maybe I would follow the same path trod by Adam Taliaferro, the Penn State player whose recovery from a paralyzing spinal cord injury ten years earlier was nothing short of miraculous.

In 2000, Adam was an eighteen-year-old true freshman cornerback from Voorhees, New Jersey (sixty miles southwest of New Brunswick), who got some playing time at the end of a blowout loss to Ohio State. During mop-up duty, Adam dived low to corral tailback Jerry Westbrooks on one of those run-out-the-clock plays. While lunging at his legs, Adam's helmet hit Westbrooks's knee, bursting a vertebrae in his neck and bruising his spinal cord. He lay motionless for minutes. Adam was paralyzed, leaving him with no movement from the neck down.

After an agonizing forty-five minutes on the field, Adam's immobile body was taken off the field on a stretcher and rushed to Ohio State University Hospital, where he underwent immediate surgery. In a situation eerily similar to what my mom heard from my doctors, Adam's parents were told that their son had just a 3 percent chance of walking again.

Rehab was a long, slow process as he realized that he'd have to teach his body to walk, one step at a time. There were many painful moments, and one time Adam collapsed on a hospital treadmill because he just couldn't get his legs underneath him. But then his legendary coach, Joe Paterno, gave him a goal: "You're going to lead the Nittany Lions from the stadium tunnel next season," JoePa said.

Eleven months after the nightmare in Columbus, Adam Taliaferro did lead his old team onto the field as 110,000 fans at Beaver Stadium cheered like crazy. Pictures of him wearing his old No. 43 jersey and walking with an uneven gait were plastered on the front pages of the *New York Times* and *USA Today*. NOTHING SHORT OF MIRACULOUS was a typical headline.

When Adam was in the midst of his rehabilitation, he penned a poem titled "When I Walk." A few sample lines:

When I walk, it's for those who prayed for me.
When I walk, it's for the tremendous amount of love and
*   support my parents showed me.*
When I walk, it's for those I never met, but sent some-
*   thing just to let me know they cared.*

What a cool poem, I thought. *Maybe I'll get to do something like that someday—lead my team out of the tunnel onto the field. I gave myself that goal for my senior season of Rutgers football.*

I was thrilled when Adam and his parents came to see me at Kessler shortly after Thanksgiving. After his mom and dad said hello to me, they quietly stepped into the hallway with Mom, no doubt to talk parent-to-parent about my situation.

Adam took a chair next to my hospital bed and talked about his injury. "One day I was lying in a room just like this when my big toe started to wiggle," he said. "I had movement! My muscles were starting to fire again, and that gave me the fuel I needed. I still had a long way to go, but I eventually learned to walk again, and I think you can, too, Eric."

Adam had brought a book with a DVD that shared inspirational stories of people who'd come back from similar injuries as ours. Adam was featured in both the book and DVD, which we watched together in my room. I was encouraged beyond belief after viewing the video even though Adam explained that there was a critical difference between his injury and mine: his burst fracture occurred at the C5 level on his spine, which was lower on the spinal cord.

It was great to talk to someone who had been through what I was going through. When I mentioned how cold I felt or was having this type of spasm, Adam said, "Yup, been there. I know all about that stuff."

Then he looked me in the eye. "I know things are tough, but I'm in your corner," he said. "If anyone can do it, you can. You're going to be all right. You're going to get back on your feet."

I appreciated those uplifting words. Adam then told me that since he regained his ability to walk, he had returned to graduate from Penn State and entered law school.

A smile filled Adam's face. "I went to Rutgers University Law School."

Adam said he was practicing law in the Philadelphia area and was recently selected to be on Penn State's Board of Trustees in an online vote by alumni. On the personal front, he was engaged to be married.

I was impressed—and saw a glimpse of my future. Not that I wanted to become a lawyer but I could still *do* something with my life and not be a burden to others.

Adam's story showed me that anything is possible. It was just going to take some time.

12

REACHING OUT TO THE PUBLIC

A steady stream of visitors flooded into Kessler during the holiday season, which helped raise my spirits, but spending Christmas Day at a rehabilitation hospital took a bit of a mental adjustment. I got through the twenty-fifth well because Mom, my relatives, and my friends brought Christmas—and New Year's Day—to me. We celebrated at Kessler with gifts, laughter, and holiday cheer.

A few days after the New Year, Jason Baum, senior associate athletic director for communications and the primary media contact for the Rutgers football program, called on Mom and me with an interesting proposition.

"Listen, I know you're not ready to talk to the media," he said, "but there's tremendous interest in your story. I got a call from ESPN today. They'd like to do a big feature on you and use it as part of their pregame coverage for the BCS Championship game." Two undefeated teams, the Oregon Ducks and the Auburn Tigers, would be squaring off on January 10 in Glendale, Arizona, in the Bowl Championship Series (BCS).

"This would be the perfect time to get your story out there,"

Jason said. "Everyone has been asking about you, but no one really knows what's going on."

My name had been in the news a few days earlier when the Football Writers Association of America awarded me the Discover Orange Bowl Courage Award. Perhaps an ESPN producer had picked up on that and decided the timing was right. Playing a football game aired on ESPN had been an awesome experience for me, so it was humbling to know that a major sports network wanted to feature me before the BCS Championship game.

We agreed to do the interview, and a few days later, ESPN reporter Tom Rinaldi and producer Kory Kozak interviewed Mom and me at Kessler. They also did on-camera interviews with my sister Nicole and Coach Schiano at a nearby hotel conference room. I'll admit that I was mesmerized when I watched the eight-minute story—long by TV standards—with the rest of the fans tuned in to the pregame coverage.

The prerecorded feature opened with slow, somber notes of an electric piano in the background and dramatic lighting illuminating those being interviewed.

"There is a difference between what we know and what we believe. Sometimes the difference defines us," Tom said to the camera, which then cut to a shot of me leaning back in my wheelchair at Kessler.

"I believe I will walk one day," I said with resolve. "I believe it. God has a plan for me, and I know it's not to be sitting here all the time. I know He has something bigger planned for me."

My sister Nicole went on to describe the Believe phenomenon. "It's almost become a state of mind. It's not even a word anymore. You believe in Eric. You believe in him," she said with a warm smile.

In the piece Tom explained to viewers that doctors initially gave me a zero to 5 percent chance of regaining neurologic function. Then Mom came into view. "I didn't want to hear about percentages because my son is not a percentage," Mom declared. "My son is my son. Nobody knows the will that he has, and nobody knows the faith that we have."

Tears formed in my mother's eyes. "It hurts for me to have to see him like this. But it also makes me so proud of his strength, so proud of the courage he has because he's not letting this get him down."

And that was the truth. I wasn't letting anything get me down. I was beating the odds every day, proving that I was more than a percentage.

The ESPN piece went on to reveal to my fans that just a few weeks earlier I had felt sensation in my hand for the very first time. I described how Mom frequently rubbed my hands when she sat by me in my room. In mid-December when she was massaging my hand, I suddenly felt something. It was a slight tingle. A feeling I hadn't had since a certain afternoon in October. Could it be? I was shocked. *Wow, it's coming back*.

"As he continues his rehabilitation, LeGrand and everyone who cares about him understands that it is a long and uncertain recovery," Tom said to the camera to close the piece. "But they also believe . . . in his future, in his fortitude, in him."

Tom's segment was a sympathetic and touching feature, filled with tears, inspiration, and the power of Believe. I watched the ESPN feature in my room at Kessler with a couple of friends and family members, and I felt really happy. It was a tremendously exciting experience because I had never been on national TV before, so it was certainly a cool thing. Mom had a different reaction: she cried throughout the entire presentation. Like all of us, Mom was still adjusting to her new life, and seeing how I looked on national TV was quite an emotional experience for her. But for me, I was just happy to be off the ventilator and get on with my rehab.

The interview sparked news because this was the first time we disclosed that I had experienced sensations in my body below my level of injury. The feelings in my fingers were fleeting, however, so we didn't know which direction we were going. The only thing I could control was the effort I put into my rehabilitation. Each morning, I mentally prepared myself to have a big day, reminding myself that I had to Believe.

I worked hard to get my strength back. In fact, if you watch Tom Rinaldi's story and compare me then to what I look like today, the difference is apparent. Back in January 2011, I had to lie way back in my wheelchair, so much so that it looked like I was seriously slouching. I sat this way for two reasons: one, I was still in a weak state following my injury, and two, if I tried to sit up straight, I'd get dizzy and faint from low blood pressure. Today I have muscle strength in my upper body, which allows me to sit up much straighter, and I can also move my head to the right or left more freely. My blood pressure regulates a lot better now than it did back then.

Within days of the ESPN interview, I made my first trip to the Rutgers campus, where I surprised my teammates by showing up for an 8 A.M. team meeting at the Hale Center. This was the first time the team was getting together after the winter break, and you should have heard the chorus of "Oh, E!" filling the team meeting room. It felt great to be back with guys I'd gone into battle with. They lined up to hug me and tell me that they were pulling for me. Their belief in me made it easier for me to believe in myself.

Nearly all my teammates had visited me at Hackensack or Kessler at one time or another, but it was nice to see them in familiar territory. Even though the 2010 Rutgers team had finished 4–8 and missed a bowl game for the first since 2004, there was optimism that the black cloud hanging over the program would make way for sunny skies in 2011.

After my visit, Coach Schiano told the media that the 2011

season was a challenge, "but it's also been something that's drawn us together. I'm with Eric. Although it's hard to see, there's going to be a lot of positives to come from this. For Eric, for his family, for everybody."

I felt exactly the same way as Coach.

Onward to Jackson

For the next three months, I continued daily rehab at Kessler. During my sessions, my physical therapists attached electrodes to my back, chest, biceps, and triceps so that my body could receive the electrical charges that weren't occurring between my brain and my muscles. They secured my hands to an "arm bike" so that I could work my arms, even though I could not voluntarily move them.

Next, my arms were put in straps and held up to about shoulder level with light weights keeping them in place. I'd try to make movements, even pushing down a few inches. All these exercises helped improve my sitting posture in the wheelchair because I was working my upper body, core muscles, and back muscles.

Throughout the month of March, I had made so much progress that doctors removed my tracheotomy, and my medical team told Mom that we should start thinking about checking out and moving back home. I could continue physical therapy on an outpatient basis three times a week at Kessler in West Orange or any Kessler satellite facility.

We understood why I couldn't stay at Kessler indefinitely—our health insurance wouldn't pay for twenty-four-hour inpatient care forever. At some point I had to get on with the rest of my life. The problem was our house in Avenel: there was no way I could live there. Our home was built in the 1930s and was clearly unsuitable

for someone in a wheelchair. It would be impossible for me to ne-
gotiate the six steep concrete steps to the landing, and Mom never
could have lifted me by herself. Even if two linemen heaved me onto
the porch, I wondered if I could get through the narrow front door
in my wheelchair.

Aunt Cheryl and Uncle Ariel heard about our plight and offered
to open their home until we figured out our plan. They lived in
Jackson, a township in the center of the Garden State. Their beautiful four-bedroom beige brick house was lodged at the end of a quiet
cul-de-sac, and it would be great to be around my cousins. Once
again, the family support would be tremendous.

At the end of March, I was ready to leave Kessler. Fortunately,
we had great transportation to get there. Thanks to NCAA insurance, Mom purchased a brand-new, wheelchair-accessible Volks-
wagen Routan minivan. The van was equipped with a motorized
ramp and a system to lock in my wheelchair to the floorboard.

When we arrived in Jackson, we had an awesome welcoming
party: Aunt Cheryl, Uncle Ariel, and my three cousins Jazmin,
Aaron, and James. Jazzy fired up the theme from *Rocky* on an iPod
while I negotiated the distance from their driveway to the front
door on an aluminum walkway that had been erected a few days
earlier. Uncle Ariel and Auntie Cheryl greeted me at the door with
the hugest smiles.

What a homecoming! It sure felt good to be out of a hospital
setting. Because the bedrooms in the two-story, 3,400-square-foot
house were on the second floor, Uncle Ariel called an audible: he
turned a ground-floor family room into a spacious bedroom/living
room space for me and an office/den into a bedroom for Mom. A
flat-screen TV was hung in my bedroom so I could keep my eye
on ESPN throughout the day. Earlier, Mom and Uncle Ariel had
decorated my room with several NFL and college helmets, a No. 52

Rutgers "Believe" jersey signed by my teammates, and a red-handled axe mounted on a wooden plaque that reminded me to "keep
chopping."

The rest of the ground floor was an open floor plan with a
kitchen, dining room, and large living room with a big flat-screen
TV and surround sound system. Uncle Ariel took out a recliner so
there would be room for me. The dining room was converted into
a rehab room with a mat table and assorted medical equipment.
The bathroom downstairs had a shower, but it wasn't wheelchair
accessible, so a temporary shower was installed in a laundry room
off the kitchen.

I could not get over how much preparation they did to turn
their home into a suitable and comfortable place for me. I was
overwhelmed and grateful for their support. Auntie Cheryl and
Uncle Ariel have always been strong influences in my life, and I was
touched by all they were doing to make me feel comfortable—and
instill spiritual values. It was my aunt and uncle who had brought
me to their church—The Cathedral in Perth Amboy—when I was
younger. I still remember the joyful sounds of gospel music on Sunday mornings.

Since my accident, Aunt Cheryl had helped me understand that
God had a plan for me. Believing in God's intention for my life and
calling on the growing spirit inside of me helped me tremendously
throughout my recovery. Sure, it was easy to get down after being immobilized, but my aunt and uncle helped me look beyond
my situation for the inspiration and faith I needed to propel myself
forward.

Aunt Cheryl and Uncle Ariel created a wonderful atmosphere
for me, and I loved the closeness of family. What a difference that
made in our lives! I was home again and ready to take on the rest of
my recovery with a newfound energy.

Because almost three months had passed since I did the interview with Tom Rinaldi, there was a pent-up demand for me to speak with the New Jersey and New York media. Jason Baum said he was trying to keep the press at bay, but he could only hold them off for so long.

"I think I'm ready," I said a couple of days after my arrival. The following morning, I was expecting a couple of camera crews from Channel 7 WABC or News 12 to show up on our doorstep, but then Mom stepped outside and saw our cul-de-sac filled with satellite news trucks as far as the eye could see.

"Cheryl, take a look at this." Mom pointed down the block.

Aunt Cheryl, wearing a red Rutgers shirt and blue jeans, looked at the film crews either milling about or readying their camera equipment.

"Oh, my God!" she exclaimed. "I have to go upstairs and change."

A legion of reporters and camera crews swarmed Auntie Cheryl's home, and they were directed to my "living room," where, once everyone was ready, I answered questions about my progress and what the future held.

I told the assembled media that six months after my injury, I had come to a better understanding with what happened at the New Meadowlands, that it was a freak play—a one-in-five million occurrence. "There's a reason for what happened, and that's what I truly believe," I told the reporters. "I was picked for this to happen to. Some people can't go through injuries like this. It would just put them down. I just believe God put me through this because He knows I can fight through what happened to me."

I really believe what I said. Then I looked into the cameras and declared, "I will walk again. I believe that."

A reporter asked if I was angry at my circumstances, although

I knew what he was really asking was if I was angry at God. The answer was no. "There is no room to be angry," I said, adding that I had to be patient through the entire process. "I'm learning because I've never been a patient person. It will all come back in time. I'm young. I was healthy, and now my body has to heal itself."

I enjoyed my interaction with the reporters and TV newspeople. They questioned me several times more—in different ways—about how I was feeling, and each answer was a variation of "fine." They asked how Rutgers had been supporting me and what I thought of the thousands of people who'd written notes of encouragement, supported fund-raising efforts on my behalf, or spoken to me personally. I answered that I was overwhelmed and humbled at the same time. The support was unbelievable, and my thanks couldn't be expressed in words.

I answered every single question as best as I could. I wanted the media to see my smile—not my wheelchair. These newspeople were my conduit to the public, and I wanted everyone to understand that I wasn't feeling sorry for myself. I wanted the public to witness my strength of courage and determination to walk again someday, all with a smile on my face and an upbeat attitude in my heart.

When the questions veered toward the future, I related how I was determined to earn that college degree Mom always wanted to get. In January, I resumed my college education by signing up for an online class at Rutgers called "Blacks in Economics." I watched the class online, in real time, through Skype, and wrote papers on my HP Envy laptop using voice-recognition software. There was a steep learning curve since I could no longer type with my fingers, but I gained confidence as I learned how to tell my computer what words I wanted on the screen.

I also learned that I could touch people through my computer. Like every college student, I had a Facebook page before my injury, which I used to upload snapshots of me in my football uniform or hanging out with Rheanne. But I didn't have a Twitter account, figuring that even my closest friends weren't interested in what I ate for my pregame meal.

That all changed after my injury, after my appearance on ESPN, and after my press conference in Jackson. From what my friends were telling me, there was all sorts of Twitter traffic out there about me. I wasn't a celebrity, of course, but I was in the news and people seemed to be interested in my progress. From my wheelchair, I saw how I could become a source of inspiration for fans around the world as well as become an advocate for spinal cord research, all through social media.

I opened a Twitter account (@EricLeGrand52) after I moved to Jackson, with a goal of posting something every day or two using voice-recognition software. It was fun to watch the number of followers rise quickly . . . a thousand the first week, 5,000 within a month, and then I hit the 10,000 mark in the summer of 2011. These days, I have around 100,000 Twitter followers, and I sometimes tweet several times a day.

My Facebook page (EricLeGrand52) has taken off as well, and today I have more than 65,000 friends. Through my frequent messages, I can inspire my virtual friends and fans as well as keep them up to date with what I'm doing.

"Getting ready to chop up the last day of therapy for the week" was one of my posts. On Mother's Day, I posted two photos of Mom and myself and wrote, "Love is sacrifice, we sacrifice for each other," which certainly applied to my long-suffering mother. I used Facebook to notify folks that they could still sign up for a five-kilometer "Walk to Believe" held on a Saturday morning at the Rutgers football stadium in Piscataway.

Tweets on Twitter have to be short, so I posted quick messages like:

- Crazy day but great day, trying to change the world day by day.
- Picture yourself beating the odds.
- About to get this work out in this afternoon, must put in the work to get the results you want.
- Might have to wait out this storm on the deck because there's no way I'm rolling to the car in this.

I also posted tons of fun pictures on Facebook and Twitter—like me at a 76ers game in Philly or Yankee Stadium, or hanging out with the U.S. women's soccer team when they were practicing in New Jersey.

I've also gravitated to a new technology called Tout, which allows me to share short videos, and each day I send dozens of personal text messages with my iPhone, including exchanges with friends and acquaintances checking in with me to see how I'm doing. In a quest to leave no technological stone unturned, when people try to call me on my cell and the call goes to voice mail, they will hear the following message:

> Hey, how are you doing? This is Eric LeGrand. I want to leave you with a quick message before you go. Never take anything for granted. Each day is a gift. It is a prize of its own. You have to go out there and receive it and enjoy it to the best of your abilities. That's what I do every day of my life.
>
> And always remember: Believe.

I love inspiring others and look forward to using today's technology to spread the message of hope.

Getting Another Message Out There

The media publicity and public nature of my injury has resulted in invitations to meet some important people and local professional teams.

New Jersey governor Chris Christie asked my family and me to come to the statehouse in Trenton. Mom, Nicole, Aunt Cheryl, Uncle Ariel, and Rutgers athletic director Tim Pernetti joined me in the governor's office, where Governor Christie told me that he was at the Rutgers-Army game and saw me go down.

The governor said he and his family were praying for me, and in his statement to the media, Governor Christie declared I had been an outstanding inspiration to people all across New Jersey, "not because of how much he has recovered, but also because of his attitude. He is extraordinarily positive about the challenges ahead of him. I am proud to be the governor of a state that has produced a young man like this."

The visit to the statehouse impressed me greatly, and it was amazing sitting down with Governor Christie for a visit. The statehouse was such an old building with so many doors leading to so many different rooms, I had no idea where I was going. Thank goodness we had aides guiding our way, or we would have gotten lost.

After meeting the governor, three New York sports teams opened their doors to me during the summer. Leading off were the New York Jets, who asked me to drop by training camp. An emotional moment happened at the end of practice when the entire team came together in a gigantic huddle with an opening left for me. I rolled up next to my former Rutgers teammate and friend, Jamaal Westerman, who was playing linebacker on the team.

"Hey, man, we've been supporting you through this whole thing," Jamaal announced to the team. "That's why we want you to have this jersey so that you can represent Gang Green. Be sure to put this up in your room next to all your Rutgers stuff." I was touched when he handed me a new Jets jersey—No. 52 of course—with my name stitched across the back.

I was introduced to running back LaDainian Tomlinson, who momentarily left me tongue-tied. He used to play for the San Diego Chargers and ran well against my favorite team, the Denver Broncos, but I couldn't help but feel starstruck when he introduced himself. I also met Jets linebacker Bart Scott for the first time, which allowed me to thank him for raising money for my Believe foundation through the sale of his "Can't Wait" T-shirts.

Unbelievable.

The New York Mets invited me to come by Citi Field, where I hung out on during batting practice and took a tour of the clubhouse. David Wright gave me his batting practice bat, and a team representative presented me with a No. 52 Mets jersey. I told reporters afterward that I loved playing baseball growing up and it still bugged me that my Little League team didn't make it to Williamsport.

But at least I can say I've been on the field at Yankee Stadium, since the team invited me to make a pilgrimage to the Bronx for a visit. Even though this was the new stadium, I could feel the history of Yankee baseball as I hung around the batting cage before the game, chatting with great stars like Derek Jeter, Alex Rodriguez, Brent Gardner, and manager Joe Girardi.

In between those incredible experiences, I kept grinding away at Kessler. It was the middle of the summer when I tweeted a photo of myself standing up with the assistance of a special metalized frame at Kessler. "Standing tall, we can't fall," I dictated to my voice-activated iPhone. After another session, I tweeted: "45 minutes of standing today, it's a whole new world being up at my height again."

I had to be able to stand before I could walk, and walking was still my goal because of my Adam Taliaferro–like dream: to lead my team out of the tunnel under my own power. But I was a realist at the same time. If I was still in the wheelchair, then that's how I would guide our team onto the field.

A couple of weeks before the Rutgers football program started training camp, my friend Mike Elchoness came by for a visit. We were chatting about the Scarlet Knights' prospects for the 2011 season, and I told him that Coach Schiano said I could pick any home game to lead the team out of the tunnel.

"That's awesome," Mike said. "So what game are you going to choose?"

"I'm not sure, but I might come out for the first game," I said. Rutgers would be christening the 2011 season with a September 1 home game against North Carolina Central on Labor Day weekend.

"Nah, don't do that," Mike said. "Save it for the West Virginia game."

The Mountaineers? I wasn't sure that was a good idea. West Virginia always brought powerhouse teams to our stadium. They were usually the team to beat in the Big East and had finished with a 9–4 record in 2010 and a No. 22 BCS ranking. Not only that, but the Mountaineers had our number. We had lost sixteen consecutive times, dating back to 1994—my first season of Pop Warner flag football.

"West Virginia always plays us tough," I said to Mike. What I didn't add was that I didn't want to become a distraction to my old team.

Mike was having none of that. "Dude, you know that you'd get the team all amped up if you lead us out. Can you imagine how much the crowd would be into it? West Virginia would be the perfect game."

I decided to get a second opinion from Coach Schiano.

"What do you think, Coach? Do you think I should come out for the first game or the West Virginia game?" I asked over the phone. The Mountaineer game, the eighth of a twelve-game season, was scheduled for Saturday, October 29.

"Whatever you want to do and whenever you want to come out will be fine with me," Coach replied without skipping a beat. "It's your call."

"Okay, I'm going to think about it."

When I talked to Mom, she said that perhaps I didn't want to wait that long. "Maybe the fans want to see you before that," she said.

She had a point, but Mike's argument swayed my emotions. I told the Rutgers staff it was settled: I'd be leading the team out at the West Virginia game. Maybe I could be the spark to get our guys over the hump and finally beat the Mountaineers.

Behind the Mike

Just before the start of Rutgers's 2011 season, Coach called with an exciting proposition: "How would you like to become part of the Rutgers radio broadcast team?"

Coach didn't have to ask twice. "Really? I can't believe it."

"Believe it," Coach said.

He explained that I could offer my "expert analysis" in the pregame, halftime, and postgame reports, all from a player's perspective. "You'll be our E-rock report," Coach said.

Once again, a wonderful thing was happening to me. I had always wanted to play in the NFL and become a broadcaster after I retired from the game, and here was a chance to get my feet wet in a broadcast setting that I was entirely comfortable with. God's plan at work, I thought to myself upon hearing the news. This would be an opportunity to live out one of my dreams, even if the circumstances weren't as I would have ever imagined.

I guess I had passed a tryout of sorts during the spring football game in April, right after I got out of Kessler. I was brought into the broadcast booth and asked to offer a few opinions about what I saw happening on the field. I found out, though, that broadcasting wasn't as easy as it looks. I mean, when you're behind the mike, you really have to know what you're talking about because this is live radio. You can't hem and haw and leave any dead air. You have to jump in there and say something interesting.

When Coach announced to the media that I would be joining Marc Malusis, the pregame and postgame host on the Rutgers Radio Network, a reporter asked him what might happen if I offered a harsh critique of his coaching.

"We'll take away his food after the game," he joked.

I've never liked missing a meal, so I don't think Coach had anything to worry about.

But I was worried about doing a good job, and I'm indebted to veteran broadcaster Chris Carlin, who was the radio play-by-play voice of Rutgers football. Chris met with me several times before the season and showed me how to handle things inside the broadcast booth and what makes a good analyst.

I would be working with Chris's sidekick, Marc Malusis, at High Point Solutions Stadium—the new name for Rutgers Stadium after a New Jersey high-tech company won the naming rights—for home games. When the Scarlet Knights played on the road, I'd call into the studio from home since traveling out of town was difficult and expensive.

My first game was the season opener against North Carolina Central. I'll admit to having butterflies as Marc and I got started, but they quickly flew away. Marc was also an old pro at broadcasting, and not only did he put me at ease, but he adopted a conversational tone as he teed up softball questions for me:

- What do you expect from Rutgers today?
- Who will be the impact players in today's game against North Carolina Central?
- What does the impact player need to do?

It helped that I knew my team inside and out, so I was basically ready for any line of inquiry. Marc and I talked back and forth, much like we were playing a game of catch with the football. I settled into my commentary role with no problems.

The halftime and postgame shows were similar in nature: Marc would recap what had happened on the field, run through the stats, and then ask me what adjustments had to be made (at halftime), or what the Scarlet Knights had to work on for their next opponent (during the postgame show). Fan feedback was great. People I ran into said they liked hearing my voice on the radio and what I had to say because I knew the players so well.

Because I was "working" in the press box for all the home games, one of the Rutgers staffers suggested putting me on the video scoreboard for our home game against Pittsburgh in early October and letting the fans see me for the first time. That sounded like a great idea, so we came up with a plan.

At the end of the first quarter, I drove myself to an outdoor landing just outside the press box, where a video cameraman was waiting for me. Our enhanced sound system cranked up "Don't Stop Believing" by Journey, which got the sold-out crowd of 46,079 whooping it up. Hey, this was my song.

As the familiar piano intro began, the video scoreboard showed a young black man with dreadlocks sitting in a wheelchair lip-synching the lyrics about the small town girl taking the midnight train going anywhere.

The crowd went crazy, and everyone loved it. In fact, they

drowned out Journey's iconic song and kept up the cheering. When I looked down at the fans, thousands were pointing their smartphones at the stadium's giant video screen and taking pictures of me "singing" along with Journey. Many of those photos were posted that night on their Facebook pages.

Meanwhile, I was on top of the stadium and feeling on top of the world. If singing along to a Journey song was this much fun, then leading my team through the tunnel and onto the field for the West Virginia game would taste that much sweeter.

October Surprise

On the morning of Saturday, October 29, Mom came into my bedroom and opened the curtains.

"See the snow?" Mom asked.

I looked out. It was snowing all right. Actually, it was nasty outside. A nor'easter causing strong winds and a mixture of snow and sleet had deposited an inch or two of the white stuff on the ground. Even in New Jersey, an October snowstorm was surprising.

"So what are we going to do?" Mom continued. "Are you sure you want to do this?"

"This is perfect," I said. "With all the adversity I've been through, how can I not go ahead?" After the events of a little more than one year earlier, I knew I could handle a little snow.

I wasn't so sure about the cold, however. My body always felt chilled, even if I was indoors with the heat on. I would be outside for a long time, exposed to the elements on a snowy, frigid late afternoon. There was no way I could avoid being cold today.

When we arrived at the stadium, it was freezing outside. We parked near the Rutgers locker room underneath the south grandstands so that I could see the guys before the game, especially my old roommate Scott Vallone. "You're still part of the team," he said, which was nice to hear. I especially enjoyed taking in the musty smell of the locker room through my nostrils, including the minty aroma of liniment.

Mom escorted me to the press box, where Marc Malusis and I did the pregame show. We talked about how Rutgers had started the season strong, winning the first five out of six games, but an unexpected 16–14 loss to Louisville the week before left the team with a 5–2 record and 2–1 in the Big East conference.

I noted that West Virginia was bringing another strong team to Piscataway: the Mountaineers were the 25th-ranked team in the country with a similar 5–2 record and 1–1 in conference play. The feeling among the players, however, was that nobody beats Rutgers seventeen straight times.

When the pregame show was over, Mom and I took the elevator to ground level, and I got in the VW van for the short ride over to the Rutgers locker room. It was rush, rush, rush to get there in time. There were stairs between the locker room and the tunnel leading out onto the field, however, so I had to wait inside the tunnel until my teammates came out for me to lead them onto the field.

Inside the locker room, Coach Schiano was doing a fine job putting the players in the right frame of mind. "Big game, gentlemen," he said. "You know the stakes, and you know Eric asked that this be the one game he leads us out. Let's win it for him!"

Meanwhile, I was shivering in the cold. I never thought about wearing a jacket—not at a moment like this. Instead, I had on a long-sleeve Nike Cold Gear thermal T-shirt covered by my black Rutgers jersey, No. 52. I had donned a red wool cap and gray gloves, which didn't do much at all to ward off the cold.

I waited for a good five minutes for the team to arrive, which seemed like an eternity. The time was 3:30, and a gray pallor hung over the stadium like a wet Scarlet Knight blanket. The stadium was half full because of the horrible weather.

None of that mattered now. When my teammates exited the locker room, my heart pounded with excitement. For the first time in a long time, I had forgotten how cold it was.

A red-handled axe was placed across my armrests to show our fans that I was still "chopping." Scott Vallone and another old roommate, Khaseem Greene, each grabbed a hold of one end of the axe as we moved forward. Coach Schiano cleared a path and then let me come out of the tunnel first.

The Rutgers fans—many of them wearing yellow raincoats or plastic slickers to protect themselves from the wet snow—exploded with cheers as the Rutgers Band played our fight song. Then chants of "Fifty-two! Fifty-two!" gained steam as I led a slow procession of teammates onto the field and toward the 50-yard line. Scott and Khaseem, along with Devon Watkis and Beau Bachety, made sure I didn't get stuck in the snow.

As we rolled out, I wanted to drink in the moment. It had been a little more than year since I last walked onto the field. Today I was rolling in with a new purpose. I didn't even feel the icy flakes hitting my face. I looked at the crowd on both sides of the field and thought about the journey I had taken over the last year—all the trials and tribulations.

When we reached the 50-yard line, we made a right turn toward the Rutgers bench. At our sideline, my teammates gathered around me for a final pregame huddle. Coach Schiano was in the middle of the scrum, and he bowed his head. "God, please heal this man!" he cried out. "Please let him walk again!"

"Amen!" the team said in unison.

Coach then broke us with his familiar chant: "It's family on three . . . onetwothree—family!"

The crowd cheered crazily as I exited the field, but from the corner of my eye, I witnessed two of my teammates crying—Brandon Jones and Steve Beauharnais. That's when I almost lost it, too, but I was becoming numb from the cold.

I had been asked to drop by the ABC broadcast booth, where Mark Neely and Ray Bentley were calling the game, and chat with them during the second quarter. Then I'd have to rush next door to the Rutgers Radio Network, where Marc Malusis was expecting his partner to help him out with the halftime and postgame show.

Before I could go up to the press box, though, I had to get warm again. I felt like I had driven into a meat locker and been locked inside for the last hour.

"Let's get you to the van," Mom said.

I rolled up the ramp into the van, and Mom cranked up the heat as high as it would go. She changed me out of my wet jersey and thermal T-shirt and put on a new T-shirt and Rutgers hoodie.

When I felt warm enough, we returned to the press box, where I drove myself into the ABC booth during a commercial break. Mark Neely and Ray Bentley had been expecting me, but I felt like I was imprisoned in a meat locker again. The reason why was obvious: the windows were wide open, and Mark and Ray were dressed in overcoats to ward off the damp cold. The freezing wind whipped through the booth, making things miserable.

Before I knew it, we were on the air. Mark and Ray, during lulls in the action, asked me how I had been doing since my injury a year previously, what rehab was like, and what it meant to me to lead the team out onto the field. I said I had been working hard on rehab, making progress. Leading my team was a huge thrill, I said, something I'd never forget.

We cut to a commercial, and a producer noticed that that my teeth were chattering.

"Do you want a blanket?" he asked.

I appreciated being asked, but I didn't want to be seen on the air with a blanket wrapped around my body like I was some mummy. Besides, the only thing that would warm me up was a hot blanket wrapped around my neck.

I stayed with Mark and Ray for the entire second quarter and certainly was impressed by their professionalism. I appreciated the opportunity to speak to the public about what was happening in my life while commenting on the action down on the field. But at the same time, I couldn't wait to get out of the booth when the second quarter was over. I flew out of there and went back to my broadcast room with Marc Malusis, who was expecting me for the halftime show.

When Marc and I were done breaking down the first half, I wheeled myself into a nearby suite, where Mom and some family members were watching the game. She could see that I was still freezing. Mom wrapped me in everything she could find: two blankets, a sweatshirt, and a hat. But I was still powerfully cold, and nothing could warm me up. Once you get a chill like that, it's a deep-to-the-bone chill, and it takes hours for the body to regulate and warm back up.

The first half had been heartwarming, though. We took a 31–21 lead into intermission as our freshman quarterback, Gary Nova, threw two touchdowns to jump-start our offense. The Scarlet Knights then carried a 31–28 lead into the fourth quarter when Coach Schiano gambled with a fake 28-yard field goal attempt. The conditions were wet and snowy on the field. This time holder Patrick Kivlehan had receiver Brandon Coleman open in the end zone, but the pass was broken up at the last second.

West Virginia turned around and drove 88 yards to our 1-yard line, fourth and goal with less than seven minutes to go. The Mountaineers were going for it. How I wanted to be out there, digging my cleats into the FieldTurf and being part of a huge stop. The Rutgers fans were on their cold and wet feet . . . until quarterback Geno Smith scampered around the right end and dived into the end zone.

Once again, Rutgers had lost to West Virginia. I was upset but not too troubled, because I was more worried about staying warm. If it had been a nice sunny day, I would have been much more upset than I was.

Mom drove us back to our apartment after the game with my teeth chattering and my body involuntarily shivering even though Mom had the heat blasting into my face. Back in July, we had moved from Auntie Cheryl and Uncle Ariel's home to a wheelchair-accessible apartment in Woodbridge, which borders my hometown of Avenel. The move brought us closer to Kessler, closer to our community support, and closer to Rutgers.

Our new place was a modest two-bedroom, one-bath apartment. Mom slept on a pullout couch in a bedroom next to mine. I finally warmed up just before we arrived, but when I had to go from the parking lot of our apartment complex into our unit, I got chilled all over again.

When we were finally inside the apartment, Mom took off my wet clothes, dressed me for bed, and put two blankets over my head. I shivered for a long time, and I wasn't warm until five o'clock in the morning, when my body finally regulated. It was a miserable night. Just miserable.

I didn't stay down for long, though, not after the reception I had received the day before. My spirits picked up the next day, and I tweeted this message:

So I left tire tracks in the snow yesterday as I led my team out next time will be footprints

But God had something planned that I never could have predicted.

Sports Moment of the Year

———

Like most rambunctious boys growing up, I wasn't the biggest reader, but I did like to thumb through *Sports Illustrated*. The stories were always informative and the photography was always amazing.

A month after I led my team onto the field at Rutgers, *SI* announced that for the first time in its fifty-seven-year history, the editor would not be choosing the image that would go on the cover of the magazine. Instead, *SI* would relinquish that call to the fans and allow them to choose the Best Sports Moment of 2011 for the cover of the year-end double-issue.

Fans were invited to visit the sport newsweekly's Facebook page to help select the cover from a pool of fifteen nominations. I guess some of the *Sports Illustrated* editors in Manhattan had seen the media coverage of my rollout onto the field against West Virginia and deemed the moment worthy of a nomination. At any rate, the image that received the most votes by December 16 would appear on the cover.

There were many great moments to choose from—ace quarterback Aaron Rodgers leading Green Bay to victory in Super Bowl XLV, a monster dunk by the Clippers' Blake Griffin, and Derek Jeter becoming the first Yankee to reach three thousand hits. Seeing my competition, I figured that I didn't have a chance.

What was interesting, though, was that you could follow the vote total on the *SI* Facebook page. After the first week, I was surprised to find myself in third place behind David Freese's World Series heroics for the St. Louis Cardinals and another "football" player—Lionel Messi of FC Barcelona, whose outstanding play overwhelmed Manchester United, 3–1, to win the Champions League title and stake a claim as the great soccer team ever.

It became obvious that social media was driving the votes. Surfer Kelly Slater's supporters got the word out early and drove up his numbers. Backing grew for Abby Wambach and the U.S. Women's World Cup soccer team for their huge upset of Brazil. Lionel Messi must have had half of Spain and Argentina (his native country) voting for him.

Then I received some help from unexpected sources. New Jersey governor Chris Christie and Newark mayor Cory Booker started tweeting about me and urged New Jersey residents in particular and football fans everywhere to vote for me. After that, my vote counts went crazy. I picked up a huge head of steam, and soon David Freese and I were in a horse race, each putting our nose out in front for a while.

Several days before the December 16 deadline, *Sports Illustrated* closed down the results tab so that nobody could see what was going on. I could barely contain my excitement because I knew I had a good chance to be the Best Sports Moment of 2011. I thought it would really be a cool thing to win, but I didn't get my hopes sky high or anything.

On the day *SI* would announce the winner at noon Eastern Standard Time, I had been asked to interview Coach Schiano for Sports New York—the first time I was doing broadcast work for a regional sports channel seen throughout the Northeast. Rutgers had bounced back with another excellent season in 2011, finishing 8–4, so there was a lot to talk about. The interview time was set for 12:30 at the Hale Center.

I was chitchatting with the producer and camera people before Coach's arrival when I noticed two people on the periphery.

"Who are they?" I asked.

"Oh, they're with Rutgers Radio," said the producer. "They're here to listen to your interview with Coach Schiano."

Mom entered the team meeting room. By this time, it was ten minutes after twelve, and the winner of *SI*'s Best Moment of the Year had been announced.

"Mom, can you show me my phone? I want to see if I won."

"Oh, I forgot it in the van," she replied. "Do you want me to get it?"

Did I want her to get it? Of course, I did. "Mom, I want to know if I won."

"Okay. I'll be right back," she said.

Mom turned on her heels and left the team meeting room as Coach Schiano was entering. It was time to do my interview; I guess I would have to wait a little longer, although the suspense was killing me.

The producer sat Coach down, the lighting was adjusted, and off we went—the tape was rolling.

I asked Coach several questions about Rutgers accepting a bid to play in the second Pinstripe Bowl at Yankee Stadium on December 30 against Big 12 school Iowa State. Coach smiled and said it was a terrific situation when your team can play a bowl game in the greatest city in the world, which I'm sure pleased the producer of Sports New York. "Getting an opportunity to play in a bowl game hosted by the New York Yankees is a great reward for our players," Coach said.

When I was done, the house lights came up. I was making small talk with Coach Schiano when I noticed Mom leave the team meeting room and return a minute later with a poster in her hand.

"What's that, Mom?" I asked as she approached us.

She gave me a bright smile and turned the poster in her right hand. What I saw nearly made me faint. The poster was a giant *Sports Illustrated* cover—a picture of me coming out of the Rutgers tunnel, surrounded by my teammates. "Fan's Choice" said the headline, with the subtitle "The Return of Eric LeGrand."

"Eric, you won!" Mom screamed. Just then, a half-dozen reporters and photographers poured into the team meeting room, and I heard the clicks of cameras and blinked from the flashes. They started asking me all sorts of questions, and now I was the one having to come up with answers.

The two guys who were with Rutgers Radio? They were actually from *Sports Illustrated*. Turns out my mother knew everything the day before, but she didn't tell me I had won. She normally wasn't very good at keeping a secret, but I guess she was able to keep this one, because I had no idea.

I wanted to do an end zone dance but settled for a big whoop-dee-doo holler. Coach Schiano looked happier than I was. The *Sports Illustrated* representatives said I captured 29 percent of the vote total, 10 percent higher than second-place finisher, Messi. Seventy-nine million people from 119 countries cast votes online for me. That was insane.

Even more insane is that I didn't tell anyone to vote for me, and I never voted for myself. I hadn't mentioned anything in my Facebook page or tweeted about the contest (even though other people did post about it). God was in control.

Gracing the cover of *Sports Illustrated* meant the world to me. It really did. That is something you dream about as a little kid—achieving something remarkable in the world of sport and receiving recognition for that moment from the most influential sports magazine in the world.

I was in awe and didn't know what to say.

It was dawning on me that I was inspiring more people than I ever could have imagined if October 16, 2010, had never happened.

13

TOUCHING PEOPLE'S LIVES

During the 2011 Christmas season, the Christopher and Dana Reeve Foundation hosted its twenty-first annual benefit gala at Cipriani Wall Street, a grand and luxurious venue in Manhattan.

It was one of those star-studded events, and to kick off the evening, I was asked to introduce the special guests for the evening: Meryl Streep and Alec Baldwin. It was a great honor to introduce such accomplished celebrities in front of a room of influential and important people, but even more so because of how much I admired Christopher Reeve's journey and foundation.

All I had to do was say a few words about my story and welcome the actors to the stage, but the event organizers wanted me to read everything off a teleprompter. Well, I had never worked with a teleprompter, and besides, I was used to looking audiences in the eye and talking about what's happened in my life and how I'm moving forward.

Throughout my own rehabilitation process, I have been inspired by Christopher Reeve's determination to give a voice to those with spinal injuries like my own. He brought great awareness to the cause, and even after his death events like this continued to support his foundation's efforts. I was glad to be a part of it.

Someone connected with the event had written a speech for me to deliver via the teleprompter, but it didn't sound like me, so in classic Eric LeGrand fashion, I did my own thing. The audience responded warmly and with enthusiasm.

When it was time to pass the baton to the special guests of the evening, I looked down at the teleprompter.

"It is my sincere opportunity to honor two of my most favorite actors out there," I said. "Miss Meryl Stree-eet and Mister Alec Baldwin. Please come to the stage now."

I'm afraid I got a little tongue-tied. I mangled Meryl's last name and called her a Miss, even though she's been married for more than thirty years.

"Miss Stree-eet" was gracious and took everything in stride. She smiled and even bowed in my direction as she and Alec Baldwin took the podium and bantered back and forth to the amusement of the crowd.

Public speaking is a high-wire act at times, but even if there isn't a net below me, I still like to get up in front of audiences and inspire people. I started sharing my story in the fall of 2011 when Alan Gross, a gym teacher at Jersey City Middle School 7, called and asked if I would say something to the students. Up until then, my public speaking had been limited to saying a "few words" while visiting my teammates at the Hale Center. The middle school would be my first honest-to-goodness "speaking" event before a live audience larger than a few people.

Middle school kids, I reminded myself, really haven't experienced much of what life has to offer—or what I like to call the "hard knocks." I decided to talk to them about staying positive when misfortune strikes and not to blame God when something does go wrong.

"I don't blame God, or Malcolm Brown, the player at Army, or anyone else for what happened," I said. "I now see life from a different perspective. I see that there is more to life than football practice, going to the weight room, study sessions, and playing in games. I think that's a good thing."

When I described the kickoff play—how I had zeroed in on Malcolm Brown only to go down, paralyzed—you could hear a pin drop. The middle schoolers hung on every word, and I think it's because most kids have never been around someone in a wheelchair. They'd never seen anyone talk honestly about the circumstances that landed him there. Nor had they witnessed a quadriplegic move about so adroitly by controlling a mouthpiece.

I left the Jersey City school children with this thought: "I will walk again. I don't know when, but when I do, there's going to be a huge party in New Jersey."

When I finished taking a few questions, the students were dismissed. I was still on the stage when I noticed a sixth-grade boy using a mobility cane in his right hand to mount the three steps.

He continued tapping and coming in my direction, and when he reached me, he asked if he could ask me a question.

"Of course."

"I'm blind," he said. "What advice do you have for somebody with a disability like me?"

I drew in a breath of air. His question caught me off guard, but when I saw that he could still hear, still say words, that meant he still had the ability to communicate, still had the ability to engage others.

"You have to believe in yourself," I replied. "You can't let anything stop you from being the best you can be, from being yourself. You have a lot going for you. You can talk, and you can think, so let me leave you with that encouragement."

I could see that my words touched this young boy, but he touched me as well. Connecting with this boy and others like him has helped me realize that my own struggles are not in vain.

I've since spoken at dozens and dozens of schools, either in the classroom or schoolwide assemblies. I always include a question-and-answer time when I'm done. "Go ahead, don't be scared," I'll say. "You can ask me anything."

Many times, the kids freeze up. Then one brave soul lifts his hand in the air to ask a tentative question—like where do I sleep? I never mind what I get asked. I like answering questions, and by now, I've heard them all.

The question I get asked the most is usually a variation of this: "Do you ever ask God why this happened to you?"

My answer is always this: "I don't ask God why because I truly believe this happened for a reason. I believe I've been called upon to help out other people, which I've never minded doing. Another reason I don't ask God why is because I know that question will be answered either when I'm walking again, or when I die and go to heaven. In the meantime, I'm trying to help a lot more people believe in themselves."

These days, whether it's an encounter with a blind boy or a speaking engagement in front of a thousand people in a ballroom, I remind everyone to believe in themselves, believe in the Man Above, and believe anything is truly possible because I believe anything is possible.

"Even though I've had a life-changing injury, I have a lot more to live for, a lot more to give," I'll say. "You just have to stay positive. That's all that matters. When I was playing football at Rutgers, we had a saying: Chop the moment. That meant taking life not day by day but one step at a time. You focus on the situation in front of you, not worrying about what's going to come after it or what's going on before that. You just handle that situation at that particular moment."

I don't have a standard stump speech. I don't recite some seven-point polished talk that I memorized in my head. Instead, I come straight out and talk about what I feel. That's why I like to arrive early so I can hang out a bit, and feel and see the type of people I'm around. Some crowds are loud, and some are quiet, which means you need to calibrate what you're going to say. You need to speak to each crowd differently. I always pray before it's my turn to speak. "God, please give me the ability to get what You want me to get out to these people today."

So far, I think I've delivered the right message every time. Mom would prefer I came a little more prepared, but I just like to pray about it and go for it. God hasn't steered me in the wrong direction once.

I hope someday to get into motivational speaking. I would like to share my story at conventions and before business audiences, reminding everyone not to take today for granted, be happy with what you have, and don't worry about the little things. No matter where you are in life, someone else has it worse than you, and that is something—even in my state—that I am aware of every day.

I'm Not Alone

A quarter of a million people in the United States live with spinal cord injuries, with half paraplegic and the other half quadriplegic. (Paraplegics are always hot and quadriplegics are always cold.) There are an estimated 10,000 to 12,000 spinal cord injuries every year in the United States, according to the National Spinal Cord Injury Statistical Center.

More than half of all spinal cord injuries occur between the ages of sixteen and thirty, and more than 80 percent of those who experience spinal cord injuries are male. They haven't received a thimbleful of support like I've been given, and I would imagine that the vast majority have been forgotten by everyone except their close family.

They weren't injured while playing an NCAA college football game broadcast on ESPN3, because you can count on two hands the number of spinal cord injuries that come from playing football each year at the professional, college, and high school level. Around 40 percent of all spinal cord injuries are the result of motor vehicle accidents, and the rest generally come from falls or violent acts, like stabbings or gunshot wounds.

Many are sent home from the hospital in a push wheelchair with a box of catheters and wishes of good luck. As I mentioned before, my situation is different because I had three different insurance plans covering my Permobil C500 wheelchair, the VW Routan wheelchair-accessible van, the restorative therapy bike, as well as the microAIR Mattress, the mat table, and electrical stimulation devices. Add them all up and you're well into the six figures.

What I'm especially grateful for is that we have insurance to pay for the daily nursing care that comes to our home. Each day, a registered nurse comes to our place for three hours and a nurse's aide for eight hours. Mom and I need every minute these angels are with us because it takes between two and three hours to get me ready each morning. It's quite a lot of work—much more than my mother could ever handle.

I'm not an eight-to-five person, so my schedule fluctuates wildly. If I have nothing going on, I'll sleep in until 9 A.M., but if I have to be at Rutgers at 9:30 or go speak at a middle school at 10:30 A.M., then Mom wakes me up at between 6 and 7 A.M. Getting me bathed, dressed, and through my bowel program is not an exact science and oftentimes takes longer than expected.

Yes, I said bowel program. In the interest of being transparent— and shedding light on something that's part of daily life for quadriplegics like myself—I'd like to walk you through what happens in this area common to every human being.

When I broke my neck at the C3 and C4 vertebrae, the nerves that transport messages to the digestive tract and bowel also got frazzled or disconnected, if you will. When you have a spinal cord injury like mine, you can't move your bowels on your own. I can't push anything out, so I must have a suppository administered to me each morning.

You can understand why I do not want my mother to have that chore. She wasn't exactly clamoring for the opportunity, either.

Only a nurse can administer the suppository and after she does, we wait. Some days things move right on schedule, but other days . . . it doesn't go as fluidly and takes a little while. I take stool softeners to help things out.

Once the suppository is administered, the nurse and nurse's aide sit me down on a specially made wheelchair with an opening in the seat and a bedpan underneath to catch falling objects. When I've finished my business, the contents of the bedpan are flushed down the toilet.

My health-care aides also wash me as I sit on the chair, and when I'm done doing my business, they make sure I'm all cleaned up. I'm finicky on cleanliness. Hygiene is important to me, and everything has to be perfect everywhere.

I like to be as regular as a Swiss train, which can present a problem when I want or need to travel. Because I can't—or shouldn't—go more than two days without going to the bathroom, my out-of-town trips cannot last longer than twenty-four hours unless Mom arranges for a nurse to come to my hotel room or wherever I'm staying.

I am grateful for the travel I can do. On the morning of January 1, 2012, I started the new year off right by flying to Denver to see my beloved Broncos play the last game of the regular season

against the Kansas City Chiefs. Check this out: I got to hang out
with my childhood idol, Terrell Davis, and we even joined the Broncos captains at midfield for the pregame coin toss!

I had never been to Denver before, never seen my favorite team
play in person, so it was a thrill being at Sports Authority Field at
Mile High. Even better, I left Denver that Sunday evening with my
iPhone filled with pictures of me with my favorite players, including
Tim Tebow. He was an awesome guy, and I got an understanding
of how people gravitate to him. I took a red-eye back to the East
Coast so that I would be back home in New Jersey within twenty-
four hours.

A month later, I flew to Indianapolis to witness Super Bowl
XLVI and the Madonna halftime show! I went as the guest of Ste-
phen Belichick, who was a long snapper on Rutgers' football team.
His father is Bill Belichick, the head coach of the New England Patriots, who happened to be playing in the Super Bowl. The Patriots
lost a thriller in the last minute to the New York Giants, my "local"
team. At any rate, Steve was able to score two tickets, thanks to his
dad, and I checked off another box on my bucket list.

Once again, that was an overnight trip that I could make because of my bowel program. Then a friend of mine, Alan Brown,
who's been in a wheelchair for twenty-five years, told me I could
change the way I do things. "You don't have to go every day, you
know," he said.

"No, I go a lot, and I'm not changing," I said.

But then some of Colonia High friends started talking about
taking a "spring break" trip to Miami in the spring of 2012. When
they excitedly described their plans for a four-day trip, I said they
could count me in. I had always wanted to go to Miami for a vacation. I knew I'd love being in a place where I wasn't shivering every
time I went outside.

As for my bowel program, Alan Brown said he knew a nurse in

the Miami area who could come to my hotel room, get me up in the morning, give me my bowel program, and get me dressed and ready for the day. The nurse's fee for working three hours, which wasn't covered by insurance, would be reasonable.

Plans were made, and flights were booked. Mom had to buy a portable air mattress because I couldn't sleep in a regular bed; otherwise I'd get pressure sores. The portable air mattress wasn't cheap, but we could use it for future trips. And we also had to rent a handicap-accessible van to get around . . . I'm telling you, there was a lot of planning for a four-day beach trip, but we sure had a great time—and gave Mom a break.

My spring break vacation could have been one of those promotions for MasterCard:

Airfare from Newark to Miami: $509
Dinner and drinks at The Clevelander: $40
Talking with Lil Wayne at Club LIV and always feeling warm for four days: priceless

A New Face

I have another incentive for traveling, and that's to be an advocate for other spinal cord injury victims.

Ever since Christopher Reeve passed away eight years ago, I've been told that there hasn't been a spinal cord injury victim in the public eye. For some reason, God has given me a platform, and perhaps it's to speak up for those who are relegated to life's shadows. If I can be that high-profile person, then I welcome the responsibility. Everyone needs something to live for, and I know what it could be for me: to encourage and educate others with my words and experiences.

I was honored to have been asked by the Christopher and Dana Reeve Foundation as well as other advocates for spinal cord injury victims to be this new voice and approach congressmen and congresswomen about budget cutbacks for complex rehab technology equipment. In April 2012, I was asked to travel to Washington, D.C., to lobby for a bill containing language supporting complex rehab technology and attend meetings and photo opportunities with various members of Congress. The bill, H.R. 4378, was introduced April 16, 2012, by Representative Joe Crowley (D-NY), a member of the House Ways and Means Committee.

Just before we were supposed to drive to the nation's capital, some sort of virus knocked Mom down, and we had to cancel the trip. In the eighteen months since my injury, she had never been on the floor like this. She had worked tirelessly on my behalf as my full-time caregiver, and I think something gave.

"There's nobody but me," she has said. "My life is not my life anymore. My life is taking care of Eric."

I was touched to hear those words. It's her unconditional love—and her driving skills—that have gotten me through the last two years. She put twenty-three thousand miles on our VW minivan the first year. It's seems like everything has been a long haul on the turnpike, and many days she's driving forty-five minutes each way for my rehab appointments, another hour to a middle school for a speaking gig, and then at the end of the day, she'll drive me into New York City for a gala event. I'm telling you, it's nonstop.

Mom has been my rock. And I'm so fortunate to have the support through the Belief Fund and the Eric LeGrand Patriot Saint Foundation so she doesn't have to worry about income from a job to pay for my care. The outpouring of support to lend her a helping hand has been incredible.

For instance, enough money has been raised to allow us to do an "extreme makeover" of our Avenel home in the fall of 2012. We

have a small corner lot, just 75 feet by 100 feet, so we're really looking forward to getting a new home that will have an ample-sized
bedroom for me with a Hoyer lift built into the ceiling that can lift
me right into bed and the bathroom. I'm so grateful because our
new home will make it easier for Mom to care for me.

She is very particular about my care. Mom is constantly making
sure that the nurse and nurse's aide are doing everything the right
way. No shortcuts. She wants me bathed and washed correctly. No
problems with the catheter. I haven't had a UTI—urinary tract
infection—since I was admitted to Kessler, and I attribute that to
Mom's and my nurses' care. I haven't experienced many of the com-
plications common to other spinal cord patients.

I've been spoiled by Mom. I'll admit that. I'll also acknowledge
that we have our moments, too. Remember, I really can't do much
for myself, so I'm constantly asking her to do something for me.
It does seem like she's constantly walking from the kitchen to my
bedroom to help me make a phone call, turn a channel on the TV,
or even take care of an itch.

That's the most frustrating thing about being paralyzed—not
being able to things for myself.

But I'm believing that will change.

14

SIGNING BONUS

In the lead-up to the 2012 NFL Draft in late April, two ESPN analysts were in regular rotation: draft experts Mel Kiper Jr. and Todd McShay. The duo makes for great television because they often disagree, and their banter is quite entertaining. They can be blistering in their opinions and love to talk up or talk down each player on their big board—the first round of the draft.

As I watched the pair jabber on and on about the NFL draft, it was easy for me to daydream about what might have been . . .

KIPER: My dark-horse pick at defensive tackle this year is Eric LeGrand out of Rutgers. He had a phenomenal senior season for Greg Schiano. They called him the "Beast of the Big East" because he led the conference in tackles for losses and reached double digits in sacks. He really upped his game in 2011. His power, strength, tenacity, and athleticism are all prototypical to play in the NFL. Because of his versatility, he's a lock to go sometime in the first round.

MCSHAY: I see LeGrand as a solid first-rounder because of
the NFL Combine. His speedy 4.79 in the forty raised
eyebrows, and in the bench, he posted thirty-eight reps of
225 pounds. He dominated every matchup in the one-on-
one drills. He can stuff the run and play any defense, but
he's probably best suited for the 4–3.

KIPER: I haven't forgotten the fourth-and-goal tackle the
kid made to save the day against in the BCS Championship game against Alabama. Eric made a big stop at the
goal line in front of a sellout crowd in the Superdome.
That wasn't easy when you're playing Alabama in their
backyard.

MCSHAY: You can't talk about Eric LeGrand without talking about his special teams play. After watching him on
film, I can assure you that this guy was fearless on kickoff coverage. Teams threw double teams at him, but he
had an uncanny ability to slip blocks and make big tackles. You use words like *intense, resilient,* and *passionate*
when you're talking about Eric LeGrand. My sources tell
me that he will be the surprise pick of the draft. They
couldn't tell me where he'd fall, just that he'll go sometime in the first round.

KIPER: The worst-kept secret circulating around the league
is that Greg Schiano wants him at Tampa Bay. Schiano
left Rutgers and took the Bucs job back in January, and
word is the two are very close. He offered this kid a scholarship to come play for him at Rutgers when he was in
ninth grade! They say they have a father-son bond that
can't be broken.

MCSHAY: For once we agree, which must be a record. I see
Schiano pulling the trigger on LeGrand, even if he has
to trade up to get him. He wants him that bad. Schiano

loves his leadership skills. He named him team captain
his senior season, and Schiano said LeGrand was the catalyst for Rutgers' first BCS bowl game ever.

Well, the only true part of that fantasy exchange between Mel
Kiper and Todd McShay is that Coach Schiano did leave Rutgers
in January 2012 to become the head coach of the Tampa Bay
Buccaneers.

Coach didn't tell me he was thinking about leaving Rutgers,
nor would I have expected him to. But I wasn't surprised Tampa
Bay wanted him. There was no finer coach and no finer person than
Coach Schiano.

Coach committed eleven years to Rutgers and thought he would
be the Scarlet Knights' leader for many more seasons. He inherited
one of the worst football programs in the country when he signed
on in 2001, taking on the challenge of leading a team that won just
sixteen games in the previous five campaigns. He was just thirty-five
years old and left a good job as the University of Miami defensive
coordinator to come to Piscataway.

After turning around the Rutgers program with several winning seasons, he felt secure enough to build a home for his family
just a half mile from the stadium. He set down roots with his wife,
Christy, and their four children: Joey, John, Matt, and Katie.

When word got out in late January that Coach Schiano was
being seriously wooed by Tampa Bay, I was stunned by the news.
But the Bucs organization wanted him, saying he was a defensive-
minded coach who had run a pro-style program at Rutgers. They
offered him a five-year deal worth slightly more than $15 million,
which represented a raise from his $2.3 million per year salary at
Rutgers.

I knew money wasn't the issue. Coach said he had several opportunities over the years—Michigan and Miami wanted him, and

he was a finalist for the St. Louis Rams job—but none of them jelled. "This time, this one felt right," he said.

Before he said yes to the opportunity, Coach called a family meeting to tell his four kids that he and Mom had decided that the family was going to move to Tampa Bay. But one of his twin boys had a question.

"What about Eric?"

The question brought Coach to his knees. That was a tough one. He had answers for all the other questions—except for that one.

"Well, Eric will come visit and stay with us when he comes to our games," Coach replied.

When Mom saw the official announcement of his departure on ESPN, she screamed and came running into my bedroom and turned on my TV. Even though I knew it could happen, I was still stunned by the news.

How were we going to "keep chopping" without Coach Schiano guiding us from the sidelines? After my somber junior season, when we lost our last six games of the season, Rutgers rebounded with a 9–4 record in 2011. Recruiting was going better than it ever had. Bigger things lay ahead.

But I understood the opportunities for Coach. He would have more time for his family in the off-season. The weather in Tampa sure beats New Jersey most of the year. Even though Coach Schiano has done so much for my family and me, this was a move that Coach needed to make. He would be one of thirty-two people who could say, *I'm the head coach of an NFL team.* For sure it was a dream job.

The next time Coach and I chatted on the phone, he reminded me that he was in this for life with me, and he assured me that taking a new coaching position in another state wasn't going to change our situation. He saw me go down. I was one of his players out there. In fact, I was one of his sons going down. True to his word,

Coach has continued to call me every week—since my injury and since he left for Tampa Bay.

Understanding that God has a plan for me has helped me get through the tough times. Well, God also had a plan for Coach and his family, and knowing that has made it easier for me to see him go off to Tampa.

Draft Time

The 2012 NFL Draft was held over a long weekend in late April at Radio City Music Hall in New York City—practically in my back-yard. There was a lot of hoopla and excitement associated with the draft, but I couldn't help but feel a little glum as I watched the proceedings on ESPN.

You see, 2012 would have been my draft year, and playing in the NFL had been my dream since my Pop Warner days in Avenel. I imagined hearing my name announced and walking out of the greenroom and being handed a team hat and receiving a bear hug from NFL commissioner Roger Goodell.

But that wasn't going to happen. As I watched player after player stride onto the Radio City Music Hall stage for a grip-and-grin with the commissioner, I became really homesick for football. I missed playing a game I had grown to love.

I was convinced I would have been good enough to play in the NFL. Nothing was going to stop me from getting there. I was primed to play well during the second half of my junior year and raise my game to another level for my final season of college foot-ball. I believe I could have proved myself worthy of the NFL.

I would never get my chance, but at least Coach Schiano would get a chance to prove himself as an NFL coach.

I was particularly interested in what moves Coach would make during the draft. The Bucs had finished the 2011 season with the NFL's longest losing streak, so there were holes in the roster. Coach and his assistants did a lot of maneuvering, making three trades in the first two rounds to get safety Mark Barron from Alabama and running back Doug Martin from Boise State in the first round and outside linebacker Lavonte David from Nebraska in round two.

Coach called a few days later and was his usual upbeat self. I had great fun talking about the draft with Coach, but there was a lump in my throat. Would Coach Schiano have taken a chance on me? Could I have played for him at Tampa Bay?

I knew those questions could never be answered. Nor could I ask since it wouldn't be fair to him. My dreams had died on a fall afternoon at the New Meadowlands Stadium.

About ten days after the draft, Mom got a phone call from Coach. She was outside Kessler, waiting in the van while I underwent physical therapy.

After exchanging pleasantries, Coach explained the reason for the phone call. "Karen, I want to run this by you first to make sure it's okay. We would like to sign Eric to a free agent contract with the Bucs."

My mom wasn't sure she heard right.

"Are you saying—?"

"Yes, we would like him to be part of the team."

Mom felt overwhelmed. "How could it not be okay?" she asked. "Eric will be absolutely thrilled if you did this."

"Well, we are going to offer Eric a free agent contract, and I'm going to call him tomorrow, so don't tell him."

"Okay, Coach," she said. "I'll do my best not to tell Eric, but please call him early because I don't know how long I can hold out."

My mother has never been very good at keeping secrets. Okay, she couldn't tell me, but she had to tell someone. As soon as she got off the line with Coach, she called Nicole. My sister could be trusted to keep a secret.

So I had no inkling what was up when Coach called in a chatty mood the following day. We were talking football when he changed the subject. "I want to sign you as one of our free agents," he blurted.

I didn't think I heard right. "Are you serious?" I asked. "You're going to waste a spot on me?" I knew that all NFL teams were limited to a ninety-man roster going into training camp.

"This is something I want to do," Coach replied. "I talked to the GM and our owner, and everyone is on board."

I didn't know what to say except, "Thanks, Coach."

But deep down, I was super, super excited. This was a dream come true. I had always wanted to go to the NFL. It wasn't the circumstances that I wanted, and I knew I would never get on the field, but this gesture from Coach . . . this act of humanity . . . meant the world to me. I also knew this decision would show football fans everywhere what type of person Greg Schiano was—someone who looked out for the welfare of others instead of himself.

Coach said he would send me a team jersey with No. 52 and my name on the back as well as a Bucs helmet, and he also invited me to come to Tampa Bay to meet my teammates whenever I wanted.

When the phone call was over, I felt like I could levitate in my wheelchair—or at least do some wheelies. It didn't take long for the Tampa Bay organization to announce the news—including a statement from Coach Schiano saying, "The way Eric lives his life epitomizes what we are looking for in Buccaneer Men." He called the signing "a small gesture to recognize his character, spirit, and perseverance."

Tampa Bay's action hit a chord with football fans across the country. My new BFF, Lil Wayne, tweeted: "Today, Eric LeGrand was drafted into the NFL. Mark this down as a beautiful day in sports." I also received eighty-two text messages and fifteen missed calls within two hours of the announcement.

Because of the tremendous local media interest in my story, Rutgers scheduled a press conference that evening at the Hale Center. Using my mouthpiece to move and steer my wheelchair, I came out onto the stage for the press briefing under my own power.

I did my best to describe the shock and awe that I felt upon hearing the news from Coach Schiano and how he had looked out for me since day one of my injury—seeking the best doctors, the best nurses, the best therapy. Coach even pulled some strings to get me cable TV—and ESPN—during my five-month stay at Kessler. "No matter what, even though he is down in Tampa right now, he is still keeping me on his shoulders and on his mind," I said. "Coach has not forgotten about me and my family up here in New Jersey."

Later, I learned how the whole free agent thing with Tampa Bay came to be.

Each year, the NFL has seven draft rounds, which means that with thirty-two teams, 224 players (in principle) are drafted. The last player picked is called "Mr. Irrelevant" because he's likely a player who'll never make an NFL roster. Every year, Mr. Irrelevant is invited to Newport Beach, California, for a roast and a ceremony awarding him with the Lowsman Trophy, which mimics the Heisman Trophy but depicts a player fumbling a football.

Mike McCartney, who helped Coach Schiano become a Christian years ago, had become a player's agent and remained a good friend. Before the draft, he approached Coach with an idea to have the NFL allow one more player to be drafted after the final pick of Round 7 and call him "Mr. Relevant" instead. The idea would be to honor a college player with difficult circumstances who wasn't going to be drafted—like someone in my position.

Coach Schiano loved the idea. So did the Bucs' general manager, Mark Dominik. But in the busy spring months leading up the draft, the tyranny of the urgent got the best of Coach. He ran out of time to run his idea past the National Football League headquarters in New York City. That's when Coach got the idea to do the next best thing—offer me a contract as a free agent, which I could sign and be part of the team.

The Bucs ownership thought Coach's gesture was truly wonderful—and so did football fans everywhere.

What does the signing mean in practical terms? There was no money involved, but the team flew me down to Tampa Bay in June during an OTA—that's NFL lingo for "organized team activity"—to watch a practice, meet my teammates, and say a few words to them. Inside the locker room at One Buc Place, my message was simple to the guys: Play every down like it's your last.

"Appreciate everything you have," I said. "Not too many people get paid to do what they love to do, so don't take for granted things that other people don't have," I said.

I'm sure speaking those words from a wheelchair carried some impact. Bucs defensive tackle Gerald McCoy told the Associated Press afterward, "We always complain about a bunch of nothing. For a guy to have the sport he loves taken away from him completely to be as happy as he's ever been, what can we really complain about? If you've never found any type of motivation before, listening to him talk is definitely a confidence and motivation builder."

After visiting with my teammates, I did a meet-the-press briefing with Coach Schiano at my side. I wore a red Bucs jersey—No. 52, of course—for the media event.

Coach opened with these remarks: "Throughout this whole time, I got to know his mother, Karen LeGrand, really, really well. She's as tough a lady as you've ever met. You can see that this is her son. I can remember being in the hospital many times with Eric, and the things that he would say to me would blow me away. The kind of selfless guy that he is. Worried about me, worried about his mom.

"Meanwhile, he's laying in a bed with tubes coming out of his mouth. He can't move. Still to this day, as he works painstakingly to recover, that tells me and tells those people that he's influencing that this all happened for a reason . . . that he can have an effect on other people and be an inspiration to them.

"I don't know if this happened to me that I could be half the man Eric is. When I look at guys and look at people who should be referred to as heroes, this guy—in my book—is a true hero and a true inspiration."

Once again, I was humbled by Coach's words. After expressing my thanks to Coach Schiano, I announced that my No. 52 Buccaneers jersey was now on sale, with all proceeds earmarked for spinal cord research and helping others who lack insurance or the right equipment with their recovery.

I also announced that I would return to Tampa Bay for the 2012 season opener against the Carolina Panthers and see the team play the following week in my backyard when the Bucs invaded Gotham to take on the New York Giants at . . . MetLife Stadium (or the old New Meadowlands Stadium). From the viewpoint in my wheelchair, I'm sure I'd be reliving a Saturday afternoon nearly two years ago.

But I knew I would be okay because of the love of my family and the thoughtfulness of Coach Schiano, who didn't have to sign me as an NFL free agent, but he did.

Thanks, Coach, for fulfilling a dream.

Another Way of Kicking Off

Coach Schiano was also getting attention for his revolutionary idea to do away with kickoffs and replace them with a better and safer way to start the game after a field goal or touchdown.

After I went down, Coach did some research and learned that the most dangerous play in the game is the onside kick, with the kickoff play a close second. He also discovered that while kickoffs account for a little less than 6 percent of all plays, 17 percent of the game's catastrophic injuries happen during the kickoff and kickoff return.

This is the main reason why the NFL moved up the kickoff line from the 30-yard line to the 35-yard line and limited the width of the "wedge"—a wall of blockers—for the 2011 season. No longer could humongous players link arms and form three- and four-man wedges, knocking down potential blockers like bowling pins. Under the new rules, wedges were limited to two players.

The idea behind tweaking the kickoff rules was to help avoid high-speed contact that lead to concussions, broken bones, and spinal cord injuries—like the one that felled me. As expected, the number of NFL kickoff returns per game dropped considerably from 80.1 percent in 2010 to 53.4 percent in 2011.

Or, put another way, the number of touchbacks increased by 50 percent. As all football fans will agree, there's no excitement watching the return man take a knee in the end zone.

That's why the NCAA's Playing Rules Oversight Panel, when they adopted the 35-yard kickoff line for the 2012 college football season, ordered an important difference: touchbacks will be placed at the 25-yard line instead of the 20-yard line.

But Coach Schiano knew that tweaking the spot of the kickoff didn't fully address the safety issue. There would still be defenders sprinting down the field and smacking into blockers and return men at full speed. Was there a different way of doing the kickoff that could actually enhance the excitement of the game? After all, the college game had adopted overtime rules in 1996, under which each team is given a possession at their opponent's 25-yard line. We've witnessed some of the most dramatic finishes ever in the last fifteen years, and few can imagine what college football would be like without overtime. Everyone loves OT.

Then Coach had an idea: if a team scores a touchdown or a field goal, they immediately get the ball back on their own 30-yard line, but it would be fourth down and 15 yards to go. What a revolutionary idea.

Let's say Rutgers was down four points with less than two minutes to go in the game and no timeouts. Under these circumstances, the Scarlet Knights would line up and go for it, probably with a pass play. Fail to gain 15 yards, and the other team has possession at the spot of the ball. But make 15 yards, and Rutgers keeps its hopes for a comeback alive.

Most of the time—I'd say 90 or 95 percent—Rutgers would call out their punt unit and kick the ball away. Punts are considerably less dangerous than kickoffs because the coverage unit is blocked at the line of scrimmage. Fewer players are making long sprints to crush the return man. Punts instead of kickoffs would lead to less impact and fewer collisions.

Coach said he reviewed five, ten years of statistical data on what the conversation percentage was for recovering an onside kick and matched that with the conversation rate of a third-down play. They generally intersected at third-and-fifteen, maybe third-and-eighteen, so that's how he came up with a fourth-and-fifteen situation. He said the ball could be put down at the 30-yard line or perhaps the 32- or the 35-yard line to encourage more teams to go for it on their fourth-and-fifteen play.

This new way of "kicking off" could create a really exciting play and give the football pundits another topic to discuss: should Team X go for it or punt the ball away?

What really got Coach thinking outside the box was an incident that happened the very next afternoon after I went down against

Army. In the same stadium, in a nearly identical spot on the field, and during a fourth-quarter kickoff, a special teams player for the Detroit Lions, Zack Follett, took a helmet-to-helmet hit. He lay on the field, immobilized, for about five minutes while a hush fell over the crowd watching the Lions play the New York Giants at the New Meadowlands. Follett was placed on a stretcher and carted off the field. Paramedics rushed him to—you guessed it—Hackensack University Medical Center.

Doctors' fears that he had broken his neck were eased when X-rays and tests showed no evidence of a cervical spine fracture. Follett also had movement in his arms and legs. He was kept at Hackensack for the night to undergo more tests and evaluation, but was released the following day.

Coach Schiano said that Zack Follett came by to see me after he was discharged—and I vaguely remember him coming to my room seated in a wheelchair.

That's two in two days, Coach Schiano thought, which got him thinking about a new way to do the kickoff. As Coach likes to say, there are no coincidences in the game of football or the game of life.

Coach told me that his idea—as crazy as it may sound the first time you hear it—is getting traction. He's buttonholed NFL commissioner Goodell, who has been vocal about protecting players in these dangerous play situations. Coach knows that a lot of football traditionalists will say, *You can't do that,* but sometimes big rule changes advance our enjoyment of America's favorite sport—and make the game safer for the players.

I certainly understand why Coach is suggesting a whole new approach to kickoff because he saw one of his players go down, but I think eliminating the kickoff would change the fabric of the game. I excelled at kickoff coverage and used to run down the field making plays, stopping the return men behind the 20-yard line. Special teams were my calling card, and I would hate to stop someone else from becoming an impact player on what is often a pivotal play in a football game.

But it's an interesting debate, and both sides make valid points. We'll just have to see how it plays out in the future. I'll be watching closely—from my wheelchair and hopefully one day standing on the sidelines.

15

MY EXTRA POINT

It's hard to believe that almost 10 percent of my life has been in a wheelchair.

When I became paralyzed, I know that many football fans thought my life was over.

They said I'd never shake a hand.

Walk across the street.

Use the remote.

Hold a cheeseburger and take a bite.

Brush my teeth.

Grab a shower.

Text a message.

Dial a friend.

Hold an iPad.

Work a jigsaw puzzle.

Walk across a room.

Hold a baby.

Those things—and there are hundreds more I could list—are out of my control. But I can do so much more:

I can make eye contact.
Flash a bright smile.
Have a winning attitude.
Continue to try as hard as I can in rehab.
Share my thoughts in a book.
Watch football games on TV.
Speak words of encouragement.
Tell others that life doesn't end when you face adversity.
Live life to the fullest I am able.
Point people to God.

Those are some of the things I can do and will continue to do in the future.

That's because I believe.

I believe that I will someday get out of this wheelchair and walk again. I believe that I'll stand and shake someone's hand again. I believe that I'll be able to care for myself someday. That belief fuels everything I do.

I don't know when I will rise out of this chair, but until then, I'll live a blessed life. I say blessed because of the support of my mother and the unbelievable care and concern shown by thousands of families and individuals. I say blessed because I can—and want—to be a source of encouragement for everyone I come into contact with . . . whether it's a face-to-face meeting, through the media, or in cyberspace.

That's why I can honestly say the last two years have been the best two years of my life. I've met some amazing people, had even more amazing experiences, and now as I come to a close in *Believe*,

I've been able to share my story with you. It's not the story that I was eager to share, but it's my narrative, and I accept that.

My story will continue, which means I should bring you up to date on some areas of my life:

- Back in the fall 2011, I started a locomotor training program at Kessler that was part of the Christopher and Dana Reeve NeuroRecovery Network (NRN) and funded by the Kessler Foundation. If you're scratching your head about what locomotor training is, here's an explanation:

  While I'm at Kessler, I'm placed on a treadmill and held in place with a harness. One physical therapist and three NRN technicians assist me: one watches the computer that controls the speed and how much weight the harness withstands; another holds my trunk and keeps me steady; meanwhile, two PTs are on their knees, manually bringing each leg forward as the treadmill "walks" me. The idea is that the repetitive motion will retrain the nervous system and regrow damaged nerve cells.

  Of all the physical therapy I do, the locomotor training program is my favorite because it feels like I'm walking again. Of course, I can do nothing to initiate the movement of my legs—at least not yet—but each time I do a one-hour session on the treadmill, I feel like I'm making headway. I have a fleeting feeling of having performed exercise and releasing endorphins.

  For five months, until May 2012, I walked every day during therapy sessions. In a sense, I was also a guinea pig—part of a study to see if someone with my level of injury could benefit from simulated walking. I was also tested for bone density, circulation, heart and lung function, and bowel and bladder care.

An interesting development happened in May 2012. After close to one hundred sessions, it seemed like I had hit a plateau, so I was told that I had to stop doing the NRN treadmill program. A week later, however, an electromyogram test (EMG) showed I was having muscle activity below the level of my injury. When the EMG measured the electrical activity of twenty-six muscles in and around the spine, technicians discovered that some nerves were sending electrical signals.

My doctors couldn't explain how this was happening for someone with such a high level of injury. This was welcome news, and the decision was made to put me back on the treadmill program, which I welcomed because it always felt good to get my extremities moving and blood circulating. When I started walking again, the technicians noticed that I was able to twitch my biceps, triceps, and even one of my fingers just a little bit.

I think it's the start of God working a miracle, and we'll just have to wait and see. Meanwhile, I'll continue to fight through my therapy every day.

■ I'm still pursuing my dream of becoming a broadcaster. I've done a pregame show wednesday nights with Rutgers play-by-play man Chris Carlin for the Rutgers Radio Network.

I've also had several interviews . . . discussions . . . with ESPN and other major networks about the possibility of becoming part of their college football coverage. The biggest thing is trying to show them my personality, who I am as a person. Sure, I have much to learn about becoming a professional broadcaster, but my agent Sandy Montag with IMG is excited about finding me a role on a college football program. We'll see what develops in the future.

■ I got my first endorsement contract—with Subway! Yes, I've appeared in TV and print ads saying, "Eric Le-Grand believes in Subway, and Subway believes in Eric LeGrand." In the past, my favorite Subway sandwich has been a double portion of ham and American cheese on an Italian role. No lettuce, tomatoes, pickles, or relish—and hold the mayo, mustard, and ketchup. I'm not a fan of condiments, but I've always been a Subway fan. When I made my spring break trip to Miami, there was a Subway across the street from the hotel, and we probably ate there three or four times.

I'm part of the Subway endorsement team that includes rookie quarterback Robert Griffin III, basketball's Blake Griffin (they are no relation but that could make for an interesting commercial), Michael Phelps, CC Sabathia, Justin Tuck, and Apolo Ohno.

■ I made my first trip to the West Coast in June 2012 when I was awarded the inaugural Guysman Trophy for being the "manliest man," at the Spike TV Guys Choice Awards. A highlight: receiving the Hollywood red-carpet treatment with all the paparazzi and celebrities at the Sony Pictures studio in Los Angeles. Two football people made it a point to reach out to me: New England Patriots owner Robert Kraft and Green Bay Packers quarterback Aaron Rodgers, who won the Top Fantasy Leaguer award that evening.

A month later, I returned to Los Angeles for the ESPY Awards, where I received one of my greatest honors ever—the Jimmy V ESPY Award for Perseverance,

named in memory of North Carolina State (and former
Rutgers) basketball coach Jim Valvano, who died way
too young from cancer.

In case you're wondering, each awards show covered
the expense of bringing Mom as well as my nurse Clem-
entine to Los Angeles. I have to say that I liked the laid-
back and sunny lifestyle of Southern California.

- I'm on schedule to graduate from Rutgers with a degree
  in labor studies. I don't know who will be happier—
  Mom or myself. I plan to "walk" with my class.

- My mother continues to be the unsung hero. Karen Le-
  Grand deserves a statue for everything she has done in
  my service. I love you, Mom, and will never be able to
  thank you enough.

Whenever I tire during rehab or the mountain looks too high,
I remind myself of this singular goal that drives me. Someday, when
I can walk again, I want to visit the spot on the Giants Stadium field
where I went down. I want to lie on the artificial turf one more time
and take a deep breath. Then I'm going to pull myself up to my own
feet under my own power and walk away.

Believe it will happen, because I do.

ACKNOWLEDGMENTS

As someone with limited physical movement, I needed a lot of "arms and legs" to make my autobiography happen. First of all, I don't know where I'd be today without my mother, Karen Le-Grand, by my side, loving and caring for me with a cheerful attitude. Thanks, Mom, for all you do, and I'll never be able to thank you enough. That's why I dedicated *Believe* to you.

My immediate family has been my bedrock throughout this whole experience. Their love and concern—as well as their investment in my rehabilitation—have meant so much to me. My thanks to:

- my sister, Nicole LeGrand Harrigan, and her husband, Kenrick, and their sons Xavier and Isaac;
- my grandmother—or Nana—Betty LeGrand, and my cousin Judyya;
- the Curet family: Auntie Cheryl and Uncle Ariel, along with their three children, Jazmin, Aaron, and James;
- my father, Donald McCloud, and all my uncles and aunts on his side of the family (Dad had eight brothers and sisters) and my cousins;
- my stepsister, Tisha McCloud, and my stepbrothers, Gene and Manny McCloud.

My lovely girlfriend Rheanne Sleiman gave me her love and support, and it's been great having these friends still there for me: Nate Brown, Joey LaSala, Brandon Hall, Ryan Don Diego, Amir Ahmed, and John and Ray Nevins. Alan Brown and Mike Elchoness have given me great advice since the injury.

When Coach Greg Schiano recruited me to play football for him at Rutgers, he said, "Welcome to the Rutgers family." Coach, you've always been there, just as you said you would. The Rutgers family includes staff and coaches such as Tim Pernetti, Jason Baum, Kevin MacConnell, Todd Greineder, Mike Kuzniak, Jay Butler, Robb Smith, Jeremy Cole, Randy Melvin, and their wives. I'm still teammates for life with Scott Vallone, Beau Bachety, Devon Watkis, Brandon Jones, and Khaseem Greene.

After I was injured against Army, neurosurgeon Dr. Roy Vingan and his medical team saved my life and did everything they could to give me the best possible chance to rehabilitate myself. My ICU nurses at Hackensack University Medical Center like Angelique, Cherise, and Jen sat with me during the night and rubbed my head. My physical therapist at Hackensack was Leah.

My inpatient and outpatient therapists at Kessler Institute for Rehabilitation deserve honorable mention for skill and patience: B.J., Buffy, Barbara, Sean, Jerrod, Roxanne, Prashad, Lindsay, Dan, Miriam, and Gabriella. I appreciate Kessler CEO Bonne Evans and my medical team at Kessler: Dr. Monifa Brooks, Dr. Douglas Green, and Dr. Todd Linsenmeyer; my tracheotomy nurse, Rolinda; my nurses Michelle, Mary, Sharon, Ricky, and Maria; Matty, my speech therapist; and my aides Humphrey, George, George, Juice, Harold, Rema, Ariel, Kerry, and Kevin. Gail Solomon helped organize all my media requests while I was at Kessler and continues to do that today.

I had friends in wheelchairs who helped motivate me while I was at Kessler: Jermaine, Ingrid, Terry, and Mike.

ACKNOWLEDGMENTS

253

I've gotten to know and work with some great people at the Christopher and Dana Reeve Foundation, including president Peter Wilderotter, senior vice president Maggie Goldberg, and communications coordinator Janelle Lobello.

In the fund-raising area, financial planners Kimberly Kingsland and Rhondale Hayward have been tremendous help with the Eric LeGrand Believe Fund. There's also a special team working behind the scenes with the Eric LeGrand Patriot Saint Foundation, comprised of parents who know me growing up in Avenel and Woodbridge Township. Jack Nevins, my old Pop Warner Coach, quarterbacks a team that includes Millie Shea, Donna Bruno, Michael Shea, Louise Wasyluk, Leigh Farrell, Tom Mangine and committee members Craig Bruno, Allison Farrell, Tom Farrell, John Farrell, Cathy Herre, Bobby Herre, Kelly Layton, Tracy Mangine, and Harry Smith.

I also want to recognize all the people who sent me encouraging notes through social media like Facebook and Twitter.

On the pro football side, I want to thank the Tampa Bay Bucs organization, including owner Malcolm Glazer and general manager Mark Dominik.

My agents at IMG—Sandy Montag, Ben Stauber, and Max Teller—are opening doors that I could never open, let alone wheel through. It's exciting to partner with you, and we'll see what the future holds.

To my collaborator Mike Yorkey, thanks for coming alongside me and helping me tell my story with great depth and emotion. Mike was backed up by Amy Bendell, a HarperCollins editor who pressed me to reveal more of my feelings.

Lisa Sharkey, the senior vice president and director of creative development at HarperCollins, was my champion throughout the publishing process. She believed in me and my story when many others didn't. Without Lisa, there would be no *Believe.*

A shout-out to Tim Tebow, who gave me a front-cover endorsement and gave us Broncos fans something to cheer about during a magical 2011 season. Tim, now that you're with the New York Jets, you just might make me a fan of the local team.

Finally, I want to thank my God—my Lord Jesus Christ—for giving me hope and eternal life. The Bible says that we will be given new bodies in heaven. Talk about something to look forward to!

IF YOU WOULD LIKE TO HELP OUT . . .

—

Suffering a paralyzing neck fracture like I did and suddenly being confronted with so many health-care needs has been a daunting endeavor. I am beyond thankful for the support, encouragement, and prayers thousands of people have given our family.

For more information, visit www.scarletknights.com/believe.